The Origin of the Incas and Their Medicine

2012 Inca Prophecies

The Union of the Eagles of the North and the Condors of the South

Author - Editor

WASHINGTON GIBAJA TAPIA

Address: Calle convention s/n Ollantaytambo - Urubamba - Cusco.

Name of the literary work: "The Origin of the Incas and Their Medicine" 2012 INCA PROPHECIES (The Union of the Eagles of the North and the Condors of the South)

Photos: WASHINGTON GIBAJA TAPIA

Email: yanapani@yahoo.com

Copyeditor: Pammela Suyo Vilcas

English translation: Augusto Murillo nopolzond@gmail.com

English correction: Alicia Komar www.sacredvalleyproject.org

First Edition: January 2012

ISBN: 978-612-00-0770-9

Legal Deposit in the National Library of Peru Number 2012-01039

Printed in: MERCEDES GROUP S.A.C.

Willoc - Ollantaytambo

CONTENT

APPRECIATION AND INTRODUCTION

I WISH MY HUMBLE AND DEEP APPRECIATION

To Juana Maria, my mother, who taught me unconditional love, which can be durable and withstand all the adversities, the years, changes and tears. And to my family for their discipline; and who illuminate my path; to all the wise Grandfathers and Grandmothers in the Andean mountains who gave me the key to access the knowledge and wisdom of my ancestors through the spiritual connection with Mother Earth and each of its inhabitants. For my commitment to share the beauty and my talent with the children of land.

I also wish to express my deep affection and appreciation to all of my fellow guides who have dedicated their time and energy to investigate each of the sacred places. I want to tell them that there are many mysteries to discover and enigmas to solve, but we are those, who, through our work, bring this out to the light, encouraging others to look beyond their limited existence in search of peace in the world. Without you, colleagues, this wonderful world would be closed to all. This world of mysteries that we could explore not only in this life, but in many more lives to come would be lost. You are sharing knowledge by building bridges of understanding among all races, creeds and cultures.

I want to express that it is in each one of us to find a way in our hearts to find what our forefathers wanted to express. They did this by building each sacred place with infinite love and respect that they devoted to this Mother Earth with a real and abiding love to nurture to the end. I am deeply grateful for this.

In this manuscript you will read about some of the secrets and mysteries of the past. This is something so easy and simple that humans need to recover in order to find happiness in the path of their natural and spiritual life. These are known as the Inca prophecies of 2012. I have researched and studied what you are about to read because it has been my passion, my constant and continuing interest in the philosophy of my ancestors. I am sharing this with you in a straightforward manner and with deep unconditional love.

Finally, I would like to say that you may not agree with what I have written, or what my brothers and sisters of the community may feel about how the world should be today. That's okay. Just use what you believe in, and what you need, because I will be constantly grateful to the universe for the connection and its kindness towards me.

Dear brothers and sisters of this beautiful universe, I hope that this book which comes from the center of the heart with a deep connection with Mother Earth and all of the Gods of the universe, delivers the sufficient warmth, love and healing found in each moment in time. I wish to share the circles of light and the profound messages that arrive to each being in existence through a gaze or with direct contact with every being that inhabits this beautiful and adored Mother Earth. She gave us her heart and grains of sand, the reason for being and our role on Earth. Through her existence, She gave the ancient inhabitants of the valleys throughout the world a fertile land, generous and with abundant love, natural resources and more.

The wise scientific people and civilizations of the past understood that their role was not to transform and alter the Earth as done today but rather to preserve it for thousands and perhaps millions of years ahead. They knew in their hearts that in time the Earth's energy could be enjoyed with unconditional love. To receive energy one must give energy, and it therefore becomes reciprocal.

Energy is simply a transformation or an evolution. They would fill and enjoy themselves with energy because they believed in reincarnation and had enough thought to ask themselves: "Why should we alter the land if we are going to live in it in many more lives to come? We are ancient beings just as everyone else on Earth."

With this mindset, they utilized everything Mother Nature had given them, such as roots, stones, straw, water, llamas, alpacas and a host of extraordinary beings that they worshiped as Gods. They knew balance and reciprocity were very important for direct contact with the heart and mind of Mother Earth and the universe. In the same manner they envisioned their healthy food and its preparation, starting with the preparation of the fields of crops, using natural animal fertilizer from llamas and alpacas. That for them was a healthy lifestyle.

For this reason they called upon the prophecy of the Northern Eagle and the Condor of the South, in order to guide their mission on Earth, and in making decisions. Their decisions would not be made thinking of the moment nor only of themselves but thinking of those born in a thousand years or more in the future. This is what I came to understand while climbing the mountains of Machu Picchu, Wayna Picchu, Putu Cusi, and other mountains like Pinku Lluna in Ollantaytambo. In planning and building their cities and stone temples, it did not matter how long it would take. What was important was how these legacies and inheritances would be seen and would inspire throughout time. Many of these sacred places are not yet finished despite the enormous amount of time they have already been in use. The ancestors first climbed these places to the highest mountain peaks on pilgrimages because these high points are places full of energy, giving the feelings of pure unconditional love, and reveal a view as the Condor of the South or the Northern Eagle would have seen in its flight.

They understood that to plan something so big, and of the future, it would be important to see everything from above with a broader vision and perspective.
And so at the start of the construction, the present moment did not matter to them. Teamwork did. Small problems were no excuse for wasting time.

Here are examples for what I mean.

1. When we climbed the summit of a mountain we could see the fireworks of a pueblo. They look small in comparison to as if we were close. That is how the ancient inhabitants saw from above, just like the Northern Eagle and the Condor of the South.

2. For the inhabitants of the Andes and the native communities in the world, these two beings represent the heart (Condor) and the mind or intelligence (Eagle). Together they create a perfect balance, something all beings of the universe need for their existence in time and space. In this way each one of us represents the body that would also represent Mother Earth or the Pacha Mama.

3. We are the caretakers of Mother Earth, as her children, and have to connect these two beings. Imagine uniting the people that developed technological knowledge with the hearts of the indigenous people; it would be a world of both material and spiritual beauty, in balance.

4. Imagine also the companies that are exploring underneath the sea at depths of 6,000 meters in search of minerals, petroleum and other things, just to satisfy their greed and wealth of the moment. Would they understand how important it is to keep those 6 million living beings under the ocean, knowing that each one has its reason for being and functionality for the life of all beings on Earth? Those who try to destroy the life of the ecosystem for their personal benefits do not see the catastrophe it will cause in time for all of the children of the future.

It is known that approximately 250,000 species of the sea are exploited for our lives. The union of the Northern Eagle and the Condor of the South is very important to reach those hard hearts and to stop these activities that threaten Life. Let's live with these creatures of the sea in peace and love and in doing so maintain a healthy lifestyle on the planet.

THE HUNTER TEACHES HIS DISCIPLES

It is also said that the ancient civilizations sensed and recognized the feelings of animals and people. In a hunt, the hunter would put his own blood on the arrow or spear as a form of asking the animal permission to take its life, and in that manner make a connection to it. The organs and skins were returned and buried with a Quintu: three sacred coca leaves which represent oneself, family and the universe. Doing this gave gratitude and an apology to Mother Earth.

It could also be true that the hunter and hunted were able look into each being in order to understand their thoughts and feelings. They built such confidence between each other in order to build what we now appreciate. To be able to understand this and to see the depths of another person would help see the consequence in doing harm to anyone. It would enable us to understand how it would affect others who love and wait for them in their homes, as their children, couple or others. This beautiful connection is something that modern society is losing.

There was a hunter who taught the art of hunting to the children in his community, because he had been chosen as the best, but nobody understood his secret to the art. The knowledge of the Grandfathers was passed to future generations of the community through explanation, weaving or pottery. This hunter decided to teach his secret practically so it would never get erased from the old traditions.

First, he would teach balance and told his disciples that one must only hunt to fulfill the needs of their families or their pueblos. He explained only once and they understood that this balance was very important. But for the children of today, this practice, as well as the notion that they made their own arrows and knives is very odd and strange. He would explain with lots of love that everything came out of nature.

He let them see how he pricked his finger with the knife that he had made of stone. He would put a small drop of blood on each arrow, which he would use on the hunt along with his silent message towards the purpose for the hunt. He did so, breathing to the rhythm of the Earth and the animals that would serve as food.

All together the children then asked what the wise grandfather was putting on his arrows. The hunter explained that it is important to thank Mother Earth for the food it gave to his family. He would ask Her to direct the pulse of his hands and send the arrow to a male who does no longer reproduce, and to let it be a clean and painless death.

The drop of blood is to show my four-legged brothers and birds that I share the pain with them and to allow themselves to become my food, a food with love and will. The show of gratitude is for the creator and the Gods of the universe to guide my hands because my real intentions are what give the true strength to my arrows. It is true that everything must be done with good intentions. So, children of Mother Earth, never forget to not put stress on your arrows when preparing to shoot, as the excessive force will destroy the real intent of our sacred arrows and our own. It is important to teach the coming generations so that they may avoid complications later. With the lack of this teaching, mistakes tend to be made, which later turn into problems within a society. It is also good to pass on to them the knowledge and the tools to know how to fish, and not just hand them the fish.

It is important to respect nature, as the ancient inhabitants did. They worshiped a flower, a hummingbird, rocks, the moon, the Sun and everything that there was, as they felt this was the only way to preserve them through time. A flower representing life could at the same time bring inspiration and beauty, and this could change our mood. The Sun represented gold and the moon silver.

12

TWO HEARTS IN ONE BEAT

I also want to say that the ancient inhabitants during the era of the Inca civilizations in each one of the sacred places, (about 360 in Cusco), were able to go beyond psychological states. For example, walking and placing their offerings on each one of the mountains and snow caps of the Andes, at more than 6,000 m.s.l. (meters above sea level.) Here mummies were dedicated to their Gods for their kindness given to their people, in return the Gods will bring good agriculture, fishing, etc.

They also gathered fruit and vegetables and placed them inside the caves to shield them from the weather and the whims of nature as a thank you for the survival of their ancestors. They knew of the love based on mutual understanding, just like with a child. They also understood how strange Mother Nature was especially when there was a need to hug her for fulfilling the miracles that the shamans and healers of the Andes where able to see in advance. For this reason, woman became the balance in society and was worshiped.

Within the components of the Andean world, women were the most affected by colonization.

Man has also suffered the destructuralization of their societies and has been submitted into diverse forms of oppression and exploitation.

However, this problem should also be noted: Colonization has broken the balance of man / woman that existed in the traditional societies. It now promotes machismo associated by a dominant ideology.

Thus, the women of the Andes accumulate ethnic oppression of gender and class, a situation which is necessary to reflect on and which is necessary to act.

Before this harsh reality, I think the people of the Andes understood that, as a being in the womb of their Mothers, they were two souls in one and two hearts beating as one. It is why there is an eternal gratitude to the Mother for the life She gave and her vision of duality and balance. There is also Mother Earth's smile that emanates through her song that comes from the rivers and winds at dawn. They understood and recognized that the Condor and the Eagle overcame their difficulties after being born from the womb of Mother Nature and thus gave her eternal truth - shelter, health, passion and warmth. They then fought, guided, illuminated, meditated, defended and balanced. In beating Time they set away from conformism; they loved, gave birth, strength, examples, grandeur and security. Then they flew, sang, covered, forgave, wept, comforted and so on. And with moral strength and confidence the Condor and the Eagle are united and flying in circles of energy past the mountains that jealously guard the mysteries of those who inhabited these sacred spaces.

VISION OF THE ANDEAN PEOPLE BY 2012

Today the inhabitants of the Andean valleys and the whole world speak of the prophecy of the Northern Eagle and the Condor of the South. This might have a relation with the prophecies of 2012 that have already begun in the recovery of the human consciousness. For them, it is not the end destruction of Mother Earth and her societies, but rather the beginning of work that She has to do for the universe and the team of 7 billion people that now reside on planet Earth. We know that ancient civilizations worked as a team, and why they created work as a team, called Ayni (I work for you today and tomorrow you work for me.) The Minka was work as a community to build schools, hospitals, roads, etc. It meant that 12 million people at the era of the Inca worked together on their community, despite their personal differences and work activities.

This idea makes us think of the billions of inhabitants of the planet today. Imagine everyone working 1 day a month for his or her community, or even once a year, in spite of their separate jobs and careers. It would stop inequality, poverty, hunger, etc. The planet would be a better place to live in. This is a tool our ancestors have taught us and that we must recover. It is also very important to reuse this ancient philosophy, as it would be like living in a community, loving one another, as one heart, like the lions or the ants that work as a team. The answer lies within nature and with what each one of us can contribute.

In the year 2012, which has already begun, humanity will begin to raise an awareness to become united. It will understand that any being that exists on planet Earth has its reason for being, and it is not in competition with others. It will be a year of much happiness, and societies will return to the years of what they were, similar to the civilizations of the past. They will use nature as a source of life, in harmony with its surroundings. They will see each other's inner selves in order to understand how to better work together. One will see things from above as do the majestic birds of the universe. We know that Mother Nature has its quirks and they manifest in different forms, such as tsunamis and other natural occurrences: that is normal for her. We have failed to plan for these as they did in ancient times by building their villages in the mountains. But we will be born again and return even if it may be thousands of years from now.

THE GIANT CONDOR TITICACA, CONNECTING THE THREE WORLDS

It is important to note that the energy of the world is shifting and is renewed every 25,000 years. It has returned to this part of the American continent on Lake Titicaca, its surroundings, the Andes, and the valleys where ancient civilizations existed, and where there are still very impressive physical traces. This energy can be felt at every step and in several different ways by each human, especially in the area called the Temple of Wilca Uta in Amara Muro - on the Bolivian side of Lake Titicaca, 50 minutes away by auto from the city of Puno, Peru. It is also present at the Temple of Kalasasaya in Tiwanaku that it is situated on the Bolivian side along the same lake.

One of the rocks at Amara Muro has the form of a giant Condor, which represents the master of great heights, known in Aymara as the Mallku: leader of all the birds in the universe. At one time, this being existed to protect the inhabitants and their neighbors from the harsh ancient times and from the rains of fire. But most important, this bird Rock represents the connection to the three worlds: the Upper World, the Material World and the Under World. It protected every being on the planet as it tried to dive into the heart and depths of Mother Earth, to later liberate us all. At the same time it showed us that Lake Titicaca is a place of pure energy in connection with every being and animal of the past and present. This is something all human beings should know today.

Amara Muro is a living energy source, which is growing thanks to the traffic of visitors and the positive intentions of the world. There are rocks of diverse forms here. One is a Rock formation of a horse, which the locals called the sleeping horse. At one point this was a mythical being along with other rocks of different animal formations and with the great white light of healing.

This is where you can find your answers or the medicine you are looking for.

Here we see the stone arches, which are the work of the ancient man in union with Mother Earth. Physical and spiritual tools were used to gather their calculations of light and shadow, in order to understand the scope of love of Father Sun and the Gods to humanity. These arcs are directed to the rising and setting of the Sun at different angles as symbols of duality. They are also directed towards the snow caps of the Andes that shine of pure white on the horizon.

Here you feel and see the union of the four elements: Water, Wind, Earth and Fire, and the natural laws of life and love. This is where it is taught to love our neighbor and other beings of the planet in a balanced way, in the same way the Gods love their children. As one flies or walks higher in life, one must always remain humble so that his words become medicine, and not something violent in his walk of life.

Water is represented by the lake. The strong and cold Wind, refreshes the soul. It also runs through the mysterious passages carrying the message of those beings of Rock that at one time had a form, but with the passage of time, was erased by the rain and Wind. This Earth is full of unconditional power of healing that today still emanates all the time. The fire of light heats the rocks and sends this energy to the heart of each one of these mysterious beings. They come together to these holy places for the celebration of peace and love in the prophecy of 2012, which has begun in its most humble levels. Few would have visited this place, but the enormous charge of energy here rises to the most needed dimensions to be shared with each physical and spiritual being on the planet.

Amara Muro was not only a gateway to dimensions into other worlds and levels, but it is also considered the home of the Sun as well as the center of a collection of mysterious beings that still fly in its surroundings. This is a place full of focused healing energy. It is traditionally called the gateway of initiation and elevation. Perhaps it was named such by those beings that understood the balance between all of the civilizations.

I want to mention that there resides a medicinal Rock in Amara Muro. Pouring water and then rubbing between the rocks gives off putty that has been used and is still used as a plaster which sucks and disperses all of the evil inside anyone who uses it. This medicine taken out of the ground is also used to paint the forehead and other parts of the body as a connection to this great and silent love of the land of healing and as a protection to always accompany those on their pilgrimages.

Every civilization had their sacred areas. One could feel their power and presence, as well as the presence of mystical beings. Anyone who comes will feel well received and comfortable. This is because our ancestors understood that this natural security would always accompany the visitor of the future, who is returning to these spaces in search of a reunion. And they were right, as many civilizations are starting to lose their true mission of pure intention. These spaces, then, guard these circles of energy for those who recognize and have access to recover their knowledge in the 2012 prophecies.

Our Grandfathers in these sacred areas relied on the sincere love of connection and unity, where there was nothing that lied against the free development of love. It is here where men and mythical beings had full confidence to feel the heat of the natural elements at all moments and to live amongst them throughout their past, present and future lives.

One heart was formed in the beginning, of pure love and wisdom. This is the tool for the future and will be used at the time of the connection between the Northern Eagle and the Condor of the South, as announced in the 2012 prophecy. This heart will open in pairs to give love and vision to everyone in order to feel and search for the true living treasure. Our world will be sincere and our walk will be to the beat of confidence because it will be the guardian of wisdom. It will represent every sacred space on the planet.

These sacred places are the best gift that Mother Nature has given us in order to meditate, and to be one, through the rhythm of the natural music of birds and the Wind. When meditating, one will attract the God of medicine in the form that one feels convenient. These sacred places are in the mountains, above the rocks, next to a tree, or a river, etc. Just feel the heat of the vibration.

To learn how to honor the truth, we have to take all the examples and tools of Mother Earth. We need to create secure spaces for others in the future. Thinking in this manner, we will be planting or providing 50% of an entire new project, just as we have inherited projects from our ancestors. We will recover the memory that will serve as a tool to make things in a better and healthier way. These secure spaces are both external and internal, where inner peace and security is necessary. We will then eliminate all that is negative and embrace a community of positivity, together with our Grandfathers and Grandmothers who are filled with pure knowledge and a divine and sacred order.

This is why in life you have to follow, see and feel those who have an abundance of knowledge and attributes. You should see if you can get infected by them and create that power of light, a giant firework. This will illuminate the world for everyone and for infinity. This is what it means to visualize the essence of the purpose - a powerful weapon of unconditional love that allows you to fly high and ignore the small problems, just like the Condor. This is what I wish for humanity: to be as the Condor and Eagle, to be well, and to have love forever.

We honor these sacred places because we honor and bless everything that we have today. This is where we hear our inner voice, or the voices of mysterious beings, or our angels - or whatever we want to call those that care for us. In order to work with humility and simplicity, we should remember that we were once small ourselves, just like the birth of a child that brings life and pureness to Earth.

Sacred spaces such as Amara Muro, Machu Picchu, Ollantaytambo, Vilca Bamba, and Chinchero, etc. awaken the thirst of giving and sharing, and erase the horrible disease and symptoms of only taking and receiving. To collect these tools and resources, we will receive only the energy of the transparent light. This will permit us to live in the future with harmony and peace as in the prophecies of 2012. The message will then be sent to the looters by exposing their insane greed. It will reach everyone on Earth, radiating outwards, just as circles increasingly expand from a stone thrown into a body of water.

It is time to demonstrate that we love with the same intensity as our Grandfathers, siblings, the Fire, the Earth, the Air and the Water. Although we are all different, we all dream, sing, cry, see, feel and walk in accordance to our true intentions of light. That is why we are all identical. We are children of only Mother Earth and God. They have shown us the way to honor all of our blessings as the five fingers on our hand: no matter how different each may look, they are united in a single fist.

But this connection with the Condor and Rock and Earth has its sacred message because it is the guardian of all living beings and of the Earth itself. It is She who stores the food and the seeds of trees that create life, so as to bring happiness through the flowers. We know that stones or flowers can change our mood towards happiness or inspiration because they come from the Earth and have their own secrets and legends. For that reason they are loved and adored like Gods and should be protected and cared for.

The land and the mountains are cared for while they sleep in the dream they share; dreaming and telling their secrets in the canyons, hills and rivers, which are a constant source of beauty. They nourish us with so much energy for our heart and have nourished the weary pilgrims ever since time immemorial. They also heal wounds and diseases with medicinal plants and rocks, which is why we should worship them. We can feel this renewing of our body by breathing this messenger called air or by eating whatever they may give us with such happiness to nourish our hearts.

UFO'S APPEAR

Many places with live energy exist in the world. I had the opportunity to feel and be in some of these places - Sedona, AZ in the USA, the Himalayas in Nepal, Vilca Bamba and Chinchero in Peru and their sacred temples and areas. Here there are sightings of flying objects or lights by the inhabitants of the communities.

I want to share with everyone that with the approach of the 2012 prophecies, there are many phenomena of amazing lights and flying objects that can be seen everywhere in Peru and throughout the world, especially around the highest navigable lake in the world, Lake Titicaca. I had the opportunity to be there one day at approximately 12:00pm. We had just finished a ceremony at the Casa del Sol in Wilca Uta with children and women of the community when we spotted a white flying object moving in the direction towards the Sun. It made circles three times, and for a moment we thought it could have been a plastic bag. Moments later, we saw two objects approaching us and they seemed to play in front of us for about three minutes. It was a very thrilling and intense energy. Then they separated and left in different directions.

At that moment I asked the inhabitants who were mostly children, "What could that have been?" They responded that they had always seen them and felt as if they were something natural or normal; they did not find their presence unusual. On another occasion in March 2011,on Amantani Island in Lake Titicaca, I spent a night with my friend Rich Geisel: geisel2663@gmail.com, at the temple of Pacha Tata. There was also a young man of Argentine ancestry staying with us. Rich came to us and said there was a light that had not moved on the north side. Together we enjoyed this light for almost five minutes while Rich recorded a video of what happened on his iPhone. It was all very interesting because we had just finished a ceremony for Mother Earth with a Quintu of coca leaves with the locals who were carving stones with their wives. You can watch this video on http://www.youtube.com/watch?v=97W5OzxI_fA&feature=related. I have had about six sightings in my 29 years of life and it is important for me to share these experiences of Lake Titicaca with you.

UNION SUN AND MOTHER EARTH, SACRED SITES

The mountains represent energy and are called Apus (Gods). Many of them represent male energy like Ausangate and Salkantay; others are a female energy like Veronica or Wakey Willka (sacred tears) in Cusco. They have many trails due to the thousands of pilgrimages that have been made to them to make offerings by dance or other payment. The community has a passion for the water of life it has given them. The energy of the water continues to move in circles so it may always run through the valleys.

For this reason, the first settlers asked themselves for hundreds of years how they could unite the Sun with Mother Earth. They found a way to do this through the shadow of the mountains that was created on the land from the light of the Sun. For them, this phenomenon of the shadow was the male penetrating the Earth so that there may be better fertility in planting and harvesting. It is also the same reason why they created the Inti Watanas or sundials in order to represent this phenomenon that created shadows in all of the temples and valleys.

It is important to note how the birds of the Andes face the mountains when they sing. In this same manner, the ancestors did their rituals and songs, looking at the mountains of their surroundings to demonstrate their relationship and connection with these sacred deities.

It is for this reason that when the people of the Andes constructed their aqueducts, they did so singing, staging ceremonies and celebrations to the water that came from the mountains of the Andes. They played music with their Wind instruments at the marriage of the mountains and the Earth. These aqueducts that connected to their terraces, much like those of Moray, called for a celebration at harvest when they offered their best products to the Gods of the mountains.

These terraces show work that was done as a team between Scientific Architects, Engineers, Astronomers and Healers, who worked with communities of thousands of men. Always in harmony with their Pacha Mama and nature, they contributed to the climate of each village in the Sacred Valley of the Incas and the legacy of Moray.

Moray was an experimental area that was used in different ways. One was the study of different microclimates; the lower terraces can be measured at temperatures much hotter than the upper ones. It was also a way to acclimate medicinal plants, herbs for aromatherapy, ornamental plants, spices and even the sacred coca leaf that were brought in from warmer places such as the jungle. Peru has 84 of the 114 microclimates of the world. This is why it is inhabited by a vast number of civilizations, making Peru the most privileged and diverse in the world.

Another use of Moray could also have been as a large amphitheatre, in which thousands of people would convene on the terraces for various activities such as music, dance and ceremonies. The location has excellent sound quality, which is produced by echoes. These activities are still performed in the month of October for Moray Raymi, dedicated to the Sun God for his contribution to agriculture.

It was also used for astronomy. The lower circular terraces were covered with clay, which prevented the water from running for several days. In this way, astronomers from throughout the region could come and study the stars – because it became a giant mirror of water. At Moray, there are actually three large constructions of circular terraces located at different locations so water stored at these other spots could show other parts of the Milky Way and the constellations.

Near the town of Maras and close to Moray are the salt mines of Maras. These mines were used long ago, and are still used today by much of the civilization as a source for extracting this mineral for consumption, and medicine for agriculture and livestock. Ancient remains still exist that are visible underneath the rocks. These belonged to the inhabitants of the valley from different times and eras. They channel water through the rocks by a system of filtration of the rainwater. This is also done from water stored in stone or clay storages, just like the Incas did. One can now see about 3,000 pools of salt that contribute to the economy of the current population.

These pools are divided among the inhabitants of Maras and their communities, with 5, 10, or 20 per family. They use them as an alternative to cultivation. The use and extraction of salt is only possible in the dry season. It is a form of work inherited by their ancestors, especially for women who, along with their Mothers, harvest the salt with bare feet. Now burros are used for moving the cargo, but surely our ancestors used llamas and alpacas.

The warm salt water comes from sources called "eyes" by the men and women that work there. They place offerings and gifts of flowers as a thank you to the Earth for all of its kindness that it has given to them since before Time. These offerings are placed in the areas of the hot and salty liquid "eyes." The water is guided to the pools by small channels. The Sun evaporates the liquid in the pools and the salt is left in the dry pool. After repeating this same process 4 times, the families then scrape the salt into one area with small pieces of wood. They then gather and transport the salt to their storage space to be treated for consumption.

The most important thing is that thanks to this generous gift from the Earth, thousands of families can live from the revenue of this resource. It is also visited by thousands of tourists who feel and see its grand mystery, and are surprised at the work between men and their Mother Earth, which has been done for so many years. The method of work is unique in the world. I would also like to note that no one can figure out the mystery of where this medicinal sacred water comes from, and that the Earth guides to the surface. This liquid strengthens the spirit of men and makes them understand that She is alive.

SAVING IS IMPORTANT FOR THE FUTURE
My grandparents, may they rest in peace, always told me that saved bread for the future is important for the future. I remember one of them saying that the families of their ancestors had to give 20% of their harvest to the government to be saved at huge warehouses, like the old barns at Urú Bamba called Machu Ccolcas, near Chinchero.

Within these barns, very large holes were made on the ground and a plant called muña was first put in. Muña smells like mint. Next, potatoes or some other product one wanted to save was placed on top of that. Then more muña was placed, before covering it all with earth. This was left for 3 to 5 years.

The function of the muña plant is to repel insects. It is the same idea as the insect repellent used on the skin. It helped preserve food for a much longer time. For example, in case of a bad crop due to bad weather or emergencies in the community, the 20% may be returned to the same family so that no one suffered from hunger.

Many barns or food deposits were built at the length and sides of the ancient territories, similar to the ones admired at Pinku Lluna hill in Ollantaytambo. They receive the first and last light of the Sun along with the cold Wind currents from the Andean mountains. Let's not forget that these civilizations came to have about 10,000 varieties of potatoes, along with about 37 varieties of corn. Today corn is still cultivated in the different highland communities of South America and the world.

So the question is, where did they gather and keep so much knowledge if they had no form of or reading or writing? That is the reason why woven textiles and ceramics were of great spiritual and sacred value. They used them to record their moods, their history, customs, experiences and knowledge of their ancestors by the figures that were woven or painted. In this way their descendants could know about their ancestors. Today this very important tool is being lost because textiles and ceramics are only made for commercial purposes.

I remember once I was walking by the hills with a farmer from one of the communities of the Pata Cancha basin. He told me of a local party where he drank lots of fermented corn beer called Chicha de Jora and that he slept in the open on the way back home. He awoke without the poncho that his wife had created for him with so much love and time, weaving all of the beautiful family history details into it. He said he was not angry at who had taken his clothes but wanted it returned for the time and dedication his wife had taken to create the poncho. "It does not matter," he said, "because I will recognize it at any moment, even if 100 years pass because each one of our families has our own style and way of weaving (AWAR) and painting." I remember later meeting him after some time and he told me that he had recovered it from a friend who had taken it by mistake.

This story brings me to a deep and interesting thought. It is for these reasons that my ancestors had an infinite amount of honesty and trust for each other. They would be able to look inside the other by their clothes and ceramics which was a connection to every woman, man and child of each family, group and community.

Everything comes from within nature, such as shampoo. This

28

natural soap, an extract from roots, is used to wash the different wools that come from sheep and the vicuña, which is their finest wool. Later the wool is dyed in a process with roots, leaves, stems, fruits, insects, rust, etc. in order to get very beautiful colors and tones. These are seen in the textiles of each community, especially those communities that still lack access to a road. This shows that each community also used their own colors for their own identity and customs. This reminds me of the four states or Incan regions and their diverse colors.

The Sacred Valley of the Incas which is guided by the Willca Mayu River, the sacred river that is born at the border between the regions of Cusco and Puno, is in turn the representation of the Milky Way and constellations. On the river banks of this river and on the meaty leaves of a cactus, grows a white insect called cochineal. Its inner liquid is purple or red. Since long ago, this insect has been utilized as a die for wool for textiles in the different communities across this wonderful valley. For this reason, they use red garments in most communities, which stand out in the open. The color purple or red is extracted from the cochineal. Then a drop of lemon is added to change the color to orange; salt is added for red. By using a mixture of components you can get a variety of shades of colors.

This insect is also exported to other countries for the development of fine cosmetics, contributing to the economy of the local communities, in addition to providing local beauty for their eyes and lives.

I want to stress something very important: in ancient times when there were no doctors or psychologists, the cochineal insect liquid was used in order to cure people and understand their moods or to find their causes of illness. The shamans or psychological spiritual healers were responsible for these practices. Ever since they were children, shamans studied this sacred medicine and mysterious practice next to their Fathers. It is still used today in its most simple form for the communities.

The method of use is to take a piece of white paper and fold it in half, then place three cochineals on it, representing the sacred number three. Work your fingers, rubbing in different directions. It is important to concentrate and connect yourself with this activity. Think about three intentions: one for yourself, one for your family and one for the universe. This will determine the energy of the three cochineals and intentions to help find the causes of the state of mind and our real mission on Earth.

In many cases my clients and I find the answers to our sadness and happiness in this magnificent sacred art, in seeing the forms of birds, animals and mysterious beings. We also understand with whom or what animal we should connect with and work united with, in order to create our balance in harmony. Do this along with using our mind and heart as tools with the prophecies of 2012 in union with the Northern Eagle and the Condor of the South.

PROPHECY OF THE COCA LEAF

We have spoken before about the use of the sacred coca plant. It grows in the jungle and reaches about three meters in height. It was used in ancient times in different altitudes from the coast to the Amazon for various rituals and ceremonies. It is important to understand that in those times the coca was never derived into other products for illegal use, but only for the pichado or chewing. Chewing the coca leaf gave people enough energy to walk long distances through the valleys and mountains. It was also used as a medicinal plant.

These sacred leaves were given as an offering to the Earth inside the small stone mounds built at paths or high trails. Even today they are observed in most roads. Through this gift of the coca leaf and stones, Mother Earth receives the wishes of these men and women. These offerings were also buried or thrown into the air as thanks for the messages already received, and to have the messages flow inside us.

I want to share something very important which is related to the prophecy of the coca leaf that the wise Grandfathers shared with me at their community of Willoc. They told me that when the Spaniards arrived, the ancient healers and the society used the coca for the pichado, to read into the future and to ask permission with the use of the three coca leaves. When the invaders came, they told the community that through the use of these leaves, the elders communicated with devils and the evil spirits of the Andes.

Then the Spaniards began to prohibit the use of this sacred leaf, removing and burning plantations whose sole use was for their towns. This account recalls that the Grandfathers fled to the lush valleys of the jungle, filled with sadness and tears because they did not understand the empty attitude of these white men towards them.

Then the light of the Mother Coca Leaf appeared in a form of a giant white coca leaf and asked her children why there were cries of sadness from the wise healers. They told what had happened and the prohibition of the sacred leaf, which was abused by the invaders. With that the Mother Coca sighed and proclaimed not to worry and commented: "My children, I will kill them myself because they will use me for illegal consumption." She referred to Cocaine.

THE CEREMONY, TRUE SPIRITUAL PATH

When I was a boy of about 10 to 12 years old, there were many colorful activities in the mysterious and great citadel of Machu Picchu together with the different surrounding communities. Residents would come to pay homage and act out these true sacred ways, translated into celebrations to their various Gods. These activities confirmed the real reason of why each sacred space or place was built. However, today for reasons of drastic regulations on economic issues, it is very sad to see the limited access and prohibited entries for these descendants that are the true heirs of those who built these gifts.

This may be the reason why there is a loss of magic and energy in these places. The music of drums, flutes, zampoñas, rattles and small incense, which were intended to purify, clean and become the messenger to share the good intentions are also prohibited. These ceremonial instruments were used in celebration from different places for the sole reason of connecting with Mother Earth. Their energy still vibrates today to the hardest hearts.

I want to share with you this beautiful experience of my life, when my family and I were with a great spiritual healer named Mama Santuza Yupanki in Machu Picchu in 2009. She is of the Willoc community and was about 102 years old at the time. Even though it was her first and only time there in this lifetime, at a place She called Mauca Llacta or ancestral pueblo, She was able to recognize each sacred space and its uses. She said that this was the place where we should live in order to keep the energy alive and send the message of unity and love to the universe. This is the only real reason why this beautiful city was built.

She said that singing with lots of joy and energy created the vibration and energy which complements and nourishes the harmony and balance of the world. In doing so the world would offers its endless richness. She also mentioned that her ancestors had believed that this was a place of healing through the energy of places like these. For that same reason, my ancestors went to the mountains for their perfect planning with a vision to be maintained over time, like the vision of the Eagle and the Condor.

It is my Grandfather and ancestors who were sent to build this place because I am a descendant of the Inca Yupanky Tupac. So surely I had lived here in my past life. Therefore my presence here is important to help in the purification of these premises. Before each ceremony the ancestors counted on the presence of the three sacred animals and representatives of the three worlds: the Serpent of the world of the dead, the Puma of the world of life and the spiritual world of the Condor.

Mama Santuza finished by saying that it is up to us to keep the energy alive in each one of these spaces, through meditation and transmitting unconditional love and unity. We must invite all energies of the world without exclusion, to establish their beliefs and way of life with ours. We can all be part of this energy that does not discriminate against anyone. Rather, it seeks unity and a secure future for everyone because we are all equal and children of God.

INTI WATANA, IMPORTANT DAYS OF THE YEAR

The sacred places built in ancient times have a place called Inti Watana, translated into Tying of the Sun, but, in reality, are faithful copies of the mountains. These solar clocks cast shadows and accurately tell the time to sow and harvest. The dates of June 21st, the winter solstice, and the December 22nd , the summer solstice, were chosen by these wise scientific astronomers of the ancient civilizations as the most important dates of the year. These rocks and mountains are aligned exactly in the direction of the sunrise. In turn, these shadows are connected with Mother Earth as an interrelationship with man / woman in the fertilization for a better soil.

Attracting the Sun was very important because sometimes they thought their material God, the Sun, would abandon them. On some months they felt very cold or their land did not supply a sufficient harvest for their community because of the low temperatures. At Machu Picchu the solar clock is the representation of Wayna Picchu, the young mountain. Its corners represent the four mountains (Machu Picchu, Huayna Picchu, Putu Cusi, Chanchani) that surround this magnificent place and in turn its sides, the four cardinal points.

On the ground to the west side is a flat Rock with six steps that lead into it and faces the Sacred Valley or the Willca Mayu River. On this flat Rock, on June 21st at about 7:15 am, is where the ancients initiated their most important people like priests, chiefs, engineers, astronomers, architects and leaders of society. Only one person could be initiated each year as the light of the Sun emitted on the Inti Watana or Sundial. These initiations were done with people who took the reins of society and who could achieve their objective for the good of the collective. Following the works drawn from 200 years to 1000 years, they were working locally but thinking globally. Projects initiated by the first settlers, such as creating channels and the construction of sacred places, were guided by the light that they felt at their initiation in this space. From the Chacra on the forehead is where they understood the way to build a society for the future, which is as seeing as the Northern Eagle and the Condor of the South. This should be the way the governments should see their projects today.

WIRACOCHA OR JESUS CHRIST, BROAD VISION

When traveling through the ancestral villages of Cusco and talking with the locals and some representatives of the Catholic Church, we came to very interesting topics such as Jesus Christ and his life. The priest began to say that Jesus was teaching in these parts on how to harvest and cultivate the land, similar to the stories Andean men and women tell of a bearded man who came to these parts, whom they call Wiracocha or Tunupa.

We understand that this part of the life of Jesus was called the lost years, when he traveled around the world between the ages of 12 and 30. With his powers he became interested in other cultures and learned from them. He had a very broad vision as the Eagle and the Condor. There are indications that he was in France, India, Latin America and on all continents, learning and teaching great wisdom and kindness to the world and about God to his village. He also understood that thoughts, race, color and different languages are not reasons for indifference and hostility, but for unity and respect towards others. Could he be Wiracocha, who taught the people of the Peruvian societies, as the Incas did, to respect the various forms of beliefs of those they conquered? The Incas were polytheists. They loved and believed in many Gods because each one of them had life and energy, which served as a healing source.

In the sacred archeological site of Ollantaytambo, the villagers talk about a face of natural Rock on Pinku Lluna Mountain. At first glance it does not look like a character of the area, but rather like a prophet with a beard. We know that the Incas and the locals do not have beards on their faces. It was said that the face on the mountain was improved and carved by the ancient people, especially on the part of the eye. They also constructed a cap worn by priests and prophets of the Incas, out of Rock and clay, on part of the head. On his back he is seen carrying a bag, which they say are the seeds of food to teach them how to cultivate and harvest the land.

Thus, in Ollantaytambo, the current descendents of the Incas call this character Wiracocha, who is the maker of the world, and who taught men the kindness of the Earth. To leave aside religion and using just logic, we can conclude that all of the references to Jesus were pure fiction. So why are there so many characters, writers and religions all over the world who mention this character?

According to information, Jesus also believed in reincarnation, as do the cultures of India and the Andes. He surely was there at one point in the lost years of his life. Cultures like those of the Incas believed in reincarnation; when they buried their dead in mausoleums there was sufficient food and clothing for the process into the passage for their next life.

I understand that one of the reasons why Jesus or Wiracocha traveled the world was that he had supernatural powers, surely just as did the ancient civilizations. But it is important to note that the teaching in every town he went to was about the knowledge of all that existed nearby. He must have felt he could do more good teaching in lands other than his own because he was always being accused and could have even been assassinated for preaching messages from the heart to the mind for the happiness of the world.

TREE OF LIFE, BEING OF LIGHT

Trees play an important role in connecting the heart of Mother Earth to the mind and the outside world. Through their roots of bright light, they bring the energy and messages from the center of the Earth. These messages are known through clear messages that each one of us feels when we meditate and cherish a great being like the tree. Through a silent conversation we can feel their energy and love like a hug towards a Mother, Father or brother.

That is why, from very long ago, they are called trees of life: because they emit the energy of life through their breath for man and other beings that exist on Earth. When we feel their shadow falling on us, it is also the connection of the Sun and the Mother Earth. As She shelters us, it gives us a home to be in, if even for a few moments.

I want to highlight with this small example, that according to modern Peruvian history, Mr. Don Jose de San Martin, who was part of the independence of Peru, slept under a tree and dreamed about little birds with white breasts and red wings. It is here where the inspiration for the Peruvian flag came from. There are many stories and examples like these that come with the connection with the Mallku or the sacred tree of life.

When humans have questions or are just not happy, they should go and find many of the answers in our brothers, the trees. In this way, many of our enigmas will be solved. The answers will come naturally, by their silence, their breath and through the inner beauty and inspiration they emit. The trees bring forth with their roots the knowledge of the heart. They expand them into the Wind and to the rest of world to reach those who wait for their beauty with a breeze. We have to walk with our children or our loved ones to multiply these connections and to understand that each one of us is also part of nature and has living energy.

These beings in the world of my ancestors' civilization were called Mallkis or Trees of Light and Wisdom. They were considered sacred and special in rituals and in daily life. If we think about it we can understand that they give us so much happiness for the world like any other being with positive energy. Normally, the bigger trees are those who keep many mysteries and store an inner light. When the leaves fall from a tree with the light of the Sun or with the aid of the wind-messenger, they fall dancing to the sound of nature, to nurture the soil where they will be reborn to create beauty with pure intentions.

To understand the Mallkis, we have to study and understand something very important. It is simply already in each one of us, so we need to let it come out and use the philosophy of our ancestors and combine it with the modern knowledge that applies today. With a moderate balance we can understand the profound balance and spirituality of those who do not talk, but with silence and beauty inspire deeply in the hardest of hearts. Just as the saying goes, silence is power.

It is true that being in nature, away from man-made sounds and lights, we can reach many states of deep meditation and can experiment with other positive states in order to connect with our past lives and make the appropriate remedies. If we require this, then this connection is very important for truly understanding our mission or intention in life. According to our ancestors, our reincarnation would have been in several different beings from who we are today. So it is very important to respect every being that exists on Earth because it will be them who will accompany us in our next life. Sometimes we recognize faces but we do not understand where we have seen them before, or have we already shared something with them in a past life?

For this reason, my dear brothers and sister of Earth, let us live in love, harmony and knowledge, in order to inherit the good for the future, as did the civilizations that preceded us. We should take care of ourselves so we may live to our normal age. It will be much more fruitful for our own future and that of our children when we will have accumulated much more knowledge. It will be like pillars that are resistant to the vagaries of nature or like all the stone buildings which we inherited from our ancestors of the ancient world.

My grandparents said that trees emit deep music. That music of the deep sleep that comes from all four sides, the East, West, North and South, as well as the center of their heart through their roots, purifies the essence of that particular sound for every being on Earth. It is true that natives of all parts of the planet say that the silent music that the trees emit is the cure for humans in general. It is why we call them Life as well as spiritual healers as one could not only be ill from the outside but from the inside as well. This is why it is also important to heal through meditation and quiet music, but there is a universal sound, which is used to heal in different parts of the world with spiritual civilizations. OM is the sound that builds unity and elevates the beauty of sound to very spiritual levels. OM in itself is a vibration, which in audible interpretation results in OM. Its sound is the most powerful mantra of all mantras.

Our ancestors knew that when the frog starts to croak, rain will soon start and that the presence of a rainbow brings happiness and inspiration. Both feel this magical energy coming from water. They understand that through water and the tree a spiritual connection is completed. This should be the same way that we should connect with nature or Mother Earth - in a mutual understanding that with each other we will be united in eternity. For this reason the tree never forgets and saves a space for each one of us on Earth. With that mutual understanding we should continue planting more trees of life.

LIFE PROJECTS, YOUR HANDS ARE MEDICINE

On this planet, which is part of Mother Earth or Pacha Mama, and according to our connection with the Gods, each of us were chosen to fulfill a special role, just like the Northern Eagle and the Condor of the South have a special role in these times with the new prophecy of 2012.

I remember when I was a child, my parents lived in a place in the mountains called Anta Nuca near the town of Ollantaytambo. There, my 4 brothers and I walked an hour to get to school and two hours on return, five days a week. Surely we did so playing along the way. At some point we felt very hungry along the way, enough to eat a whole calf between the five of us. As children, we had to fulfill the role of schoolchildren to learn the other tools of life that were important to my parents for the future.

It was for this reason that my brothers and I understood the sacrifices we had at this stage of our lives. We understood why we felt hunger. We also understood the inclement weather as well, which children of all ages from different communities of the Andes still experience today. These experiences which were chosen for us gave us the opportunity to comprehend things and helped us to open a diner called, "The Restaurant of the Hearts of the World." Some very important people in our lives have helped support its operation for 10 years now.

As with this opportunity, we were always lucky to do different projects in communities inside the district of Ollantaytambo. Our projects come from our hearts. We do not think about this very moment, but of the future of the families that have difficulties in their life today. Certainly these children will grow up using this tool to help their neighbors. Just as the saying goes; Teach them to fish and do not hand them the fish. For more information about the different projects you can visit the website: www.pathoftheheart.org.

It is important to understand that many of the stages of life which are marked with deep wounds, as impure as they may seem, are powerful tools to use in order to help others in the same situations. For that reason, destiny, or divine God, put us in these paths to make us stronger in the spiritual and the material part. It is similar to the stonewalls in Saqsayhuaman, that stand through time. My sacred ancestors said that each life is an opportunity to prepare us for the next one. Who knows what else we will experience that will contribute to the positive aspects of spirituality in time.

Grandfather Fire tells us that each one of us has the same age as of the universe, born in different beings and spaces in time. He also says that the age of the universe is the sum of all the beings on Earth - from the smallest microbe to the largest being.

And so the Grandfather Fire, the Condor and the Eagle say to never accuse yourself or plan to make yourself feel bad. Always look with a positive perspective, and what they say of you for the work you do is not important. The truth is in you and in your heart and no one will understand your deep reasons. These are your own experiences and your life that show you your path to do good for others. The spirits say: when we reincarnate into the next life we no longer need to think and spend time on small details and thoughts that do not support us with good intentions. We will think like the civilizations of the past - that everything was for the future.

We always take life with lots of love and true feelings, connecting with everyone that we see. That is why pilgrimages are very important to help understand that we are not alone on Earth and that there is so much more to discover. Within us is the success or failure of something, not only in the material but in the spiritual as well. That is the core of life. Grandfather Fire and the Water say that the best happiness and experiences are not things, but the moment of inspiration that we breathe in with such confidence. We translate this into sharing with others in need. For this reason our ancestors made pilgrimages on different paths, such as on what is known today as the Inca trail. Here, an endless amount of temples and altars exist for meditation at higher than 4,215 m.s.l. Upon reaching the destination of Machu Picchu one has the great feeling of receiving new energies.

Along both banks of the sacred river of Willca Mayu, there are two paths which lead to Machu Picchu in about 12 hours, from Km 82 and other towns. This four-day long trail through the mountains that thousands of tourists take today has the intention of a sacred and profound walk.

Actions such as these help heal those by connecting with their past selves in order to cure the defects that they carry within themselves. These defects are mostly the cause of some mistake we encounter in daily life and do not understand the reasons for its actions. We know it is possible to heal because many have experienced it and have helped the others to do so. To understand that we have a mission is the purification of Earth with ourselves. Let's not forget that we are all sacred healers because the kindness and wisdom of the Earth is in each one of us. Discover it and begin to heal; your hands are powerful.

One way our spiritual Grandfathers talked about healing is that when you sleep, you live your inner life. At most times, you reach the reality of your past lives in your sleep. It is here that we can remove the negative and replace it with the positive of life. For this same reason I recommend that when we have an object that we create, it is very important and sacred that we use it as a tool for healing. It does not matter if it is small. A pebble found in nature with so much happiness and inspiration should be put in a glass of salty water at least once a month to remove the bad energies and to purify it. According to my ancestors, the moon and everything has life, but they can also have a dark side. The interior of all beings on the planet can be feminine or masculine. The ancestors understood that by doing good with it, it would bring joy. As a shooting star brings light and mystery by asking for a wish, it will be fulfilled because even though this star appears only as light it also has its other side filled with life and happiness.

GET READY FOR POSITIVE CHANGE, AGE IS NOT IMPORTANT

The Grandfathers who live in the mountains of the Andes have a unique connection with the heart of the land. That is why, as an instinct they listen to the voices that come with the sound of the Wind, water and the rest of the elements. They also understand that changes come upon Earth by the union of the Condor and the Eagle. This comes to transform us to what we used to be. This is something very good and positive. But they say it rains now where it should not rain, the Wind blows where it should not and there is more snow where there should not be.

I once heard a wise woman of the Andes say that the Sun and the moon are not walking in a straight line as before, but rather moving from one place to another. It is as if they are preparing for the changes to come on Earth and the universe. Something that is spoken in all cultures of the world is the prophecy of 2012. This change will be spiritually, as the conscience of every single being will come to understand that it is important to recover the simple tools of love. Being prepared is important.

There are simple but very important details in the different communities that are the descendants of the past civilization. Age is not important. What is important is what we leave behind and plan for the future. The civilizations that preceded us thought in this way. This is why they dragged an immense Rock from the quarries of Cachicata to Ollantaytambo, 7 kilometers away, or to Saqsayhuaman, or to the almost 360 sacred ruins that exist as temples or huacas. One could imagine that it took many years to carry a single stone of 180 tons. Yet, there are many carved stones in each of these quarries, which never finished getting transported. Or did they let each generation or civilization of different times continue what was planned and provide their influence on these great projects of time? An example is the great channels of the sacred river of Willca Mayu, which was made at different times, little by little. These and other mega projects are still admired even with the technology of today.

The Grandfathers who lived in nature, in the mountains and in the deep Amazon, did not know their age because it is something that was not very important for them; they had a very unique way of seeing life.

1. The wise Grandfathers who inherited the magic of their ancestors say that the ages of 0 to 20 years are considered children, who learn the wisdom of the Earth and the universe, to be guided by her and not stumble in the different stages of their lives. So that up to the age of 20 there are contacts with imaginary friends and beings that guide your growth. They are your spirit guides. The Grandfathers say the Gods of the universe and of the Earth send emissaries to guide us along our Path.

2. The spiritual Grandfathers say the ages of 21 to 40 are considered adolescents. Our eyes open and are clear to

understand the dimension of our lives and where abilities emerge to gain access to another level. It is the age when we can also transmit psychic messages to help others.

3. The Grandfathers say that the ages of 41 to 60 are young adults, in which we should all unite in thought to help and connect with our ancestors. At this age we can teach many things to mankind and can provide music and vision that can shake the hearts and ears of all beings on the planet. This will be a common message for the human race in particular, which is bound to feel and receive the positive changes of the universe for this new era. It is the age to abandon our close vision and look at our lives from a perspective that would offer a global appreciation of everything. It is a time to speak to our family members closely and see the horizon and the general plans as in several paths in and out of the voyage. In this way we can organize everything.

4. The Grandfathers say that the ages of 61 to 80 years are the matured person. At that time, we learn from the previous stages. This is where we develop the human potential to prepare for the next phase. One of the tools that we use at this stage is memory for our growth, change and desire for everything. It is here where this path starts, where all mysteries are resolved and are within our reach.

This is where we must keep alive our potential and do the rituals that connect us to the Northern Eagle and the Condor of the South and help ourselves with strength to leave the nest to join the comfort zone. It is a time to also develop our talents with the help of those from a higher level, in order to fly together as one team and heart; to accept each other regardless of others' thoughts and use their positive intention to build confidence for everyone to find liberty.

5. The Grandfathers say the ages of 81 to 100 years are all scholars, healers and have the experience of all levels of energy. They understand life and express the unconditional faith of men to the Gods of the universe, mixing the innocence of the first level to reach the levels of energy. Here also at this level is Grandfather Fire, Water and the Trees. The Trees have caused many miraculous cures because each branch is a source of energy with various connections. This phase of life is full of energy sources and understanding. Also, it is important to use the energy of the hands for the healing of the heart and mind through God's messages.

The Northern Eagle and the Condor of the South fly together

An Andean Child

Giant Hummingbird of the Sacred Valley - Cusco

Natural Corn   Tree Root

Llamas of Machu Picchu.

The Putu Cusi Mysterious Mountain

Mother Moon

The Three Sacred Coca Leaves as an Offering to Mother Earth

Agriculture in the Andean World

Learning to Fish

Love the Mountains

Their Stories, Customs, Experiences and Wisdom of their Ancestors

Children of the Future

The community Quechua Taquile is an island of Lake Titicaca where it persists in the spirit of connection with nature.

Amara Muro Rock Wall is Shaped like a Giant Condor - Lake Titicaca

The presence of a Rock in the shape of a horse which locals call the horse
Amara Muro asleep Wall - Lake Titicaca.

Amara Muro House Sun Wall   Mother Earth Rock Chinchero

Andean spiritual ceremony, an offering to the Earth with ancient
art and music.

Tree of Life in Connection with the Heart of Mother Earth.

The Sundial at Machu Picchu, One of the Greatest Mysteries of the Inca Culture

These terraces show a team effort between scientists, architects, engineers, astronomers and healers, in harmony with Pacha Mama and nature.

The Maras, which was and is used by Many Civilizations.

Huge Food Barns or Warehouses in Ollantaytambo

Medicinal plants - Muña Mint, Carminative and Stomachic Properties.

Chinchero Potato Plantations

The Sacred Uses of Cochineal Insect

Natural Shampoo Roots of Plants, Used by Andean Families

Beautiful experience of my life. I was with a great spiritual healer named
Mama Santuza Yupanki of 102 years or so in the year 2009 in Machu
Picchu. This is Willoc Community - Ollantaytambo.

Projects for Families of the communities with the sale of this book

Chickens for native Communities

Biscocho Hot Chocolate at Christmas for Kids

Books Become Blankets for Children in the Cold of the Andes

PLANTS, TEACHERS OF NATURAL MEDICINE

In ancient civilizations all over the continent, miraculous healings have been produced. A well-known example is with Jesus Christ, in his journey around the world. In the towns and communities of the Andes, groups of wise men and women have used unconditional faith and meditation to move mountains and make rocks walks. They have removed tumors and cured diseases in union with plants in a matter of seconds. Imagine a massive group bringing together their vision and focus on a single mission. It is possible to do all of this and more. A clear example is in civilizations of the past around the world, because they understood that their mission must be completed, just like water from the rivers arrives at the ocean.

The wise Grandfathers always wanted the universe to be very well as they lived. So they put it in our hands to send our personal or group prayers to all corners of the world, for everyone to hear the call in their hearts. This will lead us to find the inner joy we have been chasing. The sacred places were used for these types of activities in our native towns: to send the cure the world needed, like the union of the Northern Eagle with the Condor of the South.

There are many people working very hard to understand the function of the mystery of life. They are living something very superficially, and living in a straight line. It is important, however, to see and feel the energy in circles. The Gods will reveal that for this reason, energy will open and expand.

It is not good to have a limited external knowledge. The inner you already knows, and it is necessary for us to communicate with it. The simplicity of the truth is only possible with the communion with nature, because the connection will bring an abundant life as a result. Human beings are forgetting many simple blessings that bring joy and creativity, such as listening to the song of birds and watching a sunrise. With these little details we are connected with the wisdom of Mother Earth. We should not forget the wonderful thing about being alive in connection with the wise Grandfathers of the universe.

Ever since our childhood in the Sacred Valley of the Incas, we have had the opportunity to connect with the aromatic therapeutic native plants, which have been our guides for healing. This is especially more visible in the higher parts of the mountains, where there is no access to roads and where modern medicine has not entered.

Mother Nature is the teacher of medicine because it has a cure for any pain and disease. For example, I have had the opportunity to see this medicine in the islands of Amantani and Taquile in Lake Titicaca, far away from cities and medical infrastructure. When you arrive there, you are received by the families and are taken to their homes. They accompany each of their meals with a mint scented herbal tea, called muña. It is successfully used for pains and stomach indigestions. There are many miracle plants like this, from flowers to roots blended with oxides. These are used to miraculously cure children and elders all the time.

For this reason our wise Grandfathers say that each type of plant has a flower and also has an aroma. Apart from being beautiful, they have an important function. The plants and flowers teach us their unique way of contributing to their societies and their similar beings in silence. For this reason I say we do not know everything. Surely, there are other mysteries that are also present in these communities where sacred plants exist as essential tools for a natural existence.

These flowers always show their beauty to Father Sun in order to absorb his love and his light. They transmit it without shame to their interior, while connecting with the Earth. By the union of the sunlight with the love of Mother Earth, we humans must learn to love the differences in shapes and sizes from a perspective of light and clarity for life.

The Grandfathers say that Father Sun, Mother Earth and all the Gods always feed each being with energy - no matter if it is a Rock or a flower. This is because we are all his creatures. The thunder of the night or day sends abundant rain, so that everything may grow in order to cure with their hearts. It is in the same way that everything feeds off the light of Father Sun.

Do not forget that humans have a lot of energy similar to the infinite beings of Earth. We can heal with this energy. We can use our heart and mind in union, and the tools of our hands. Never fear that humans are less perfect, or blame others who are confused, because singularity and beauty is found in all elements of creation.

For this reason, ancient civilizations also had their technology. They studied or were connected with each plant or being, through their hearts in a direct and sincere manner. This had very positive purposes for each of them. Even in their descendants, you can see how great and wonderful the passion and the connection they have with these beings that do not speak but that do miracles of all types. The Grandfathers say that magic in healing still exists but you have to fly like the Northern Eagle and the Condor of the South in order to find it in its essence, and then share it. This is the opportunity to use the heart as it was used in the communities.

It is important to note that there is no competition between man and any being of the planet. Instead, reciprocity is important between them. When taking any being for medical or other use, it is important to correspond to Earth this energy that was shared with us. This also translates as the search for the wisdom.

Those who do not seek medical wisdom are stubborn and it is their own folly because plants do not show anything personal. Rather, they share their spiritual delight with us, their brothers. They show a respect for us and for that reason share their energy with us in a free and voluntary manner. In return, they only search for the union of two hearts that love each other.

The Gods and Mother Earth have given all beings on the planet the opportunity to grow spiritually beyond limitations. We are, therefore, at the same time the guardians of love and wisdom in search of balance that opens the way for healing and personal growth.

Never forget that all beings are endowed with wisdom, which is important to share at all times. All capacity to develop depends on the willingness of each of us forgetting fear, vanity and things that are not required in the search for the tools for the divine healing of Earth.

For this reason, all plants are Gods of the universe. By talking to them feel their heat, vibration and greatness of this silent world. Then venture out in search of the truth because silence is the power of the strong. That is why our ancestors said that loneliness pursues those who have forgotten the love of their loved ones, the animals, plants, rocks, the sky and Mother Earth. We should feel and remember in our hearts and our minds that every being on Earth from the most simple are always there, waiting to share with us the beauty of the natural world. Rediscovering or connecting ourselves with them, their powers and company will never make us feel alone.

RECIPROCITY, BALANCE OF SOCIETY

While traveling through different ancestral places, I learned that the men that preceded us for thousands of years understood that reciprocity was important for the balance of societies with other beings. Once, I was in the Salkantay Valley with a Masamas group from Oregon, USA. Our horse caretaker, who was born in the communities, and was of Quechua origin, fished trout, hunted dear and mountain rabbit to share with the others in the group. But before eating them, this man took a few coca leaves, together with the skin and intestines, and buried them as an offering to Mother Earth for sharing her love with each one of us. On many occasions our brothers and sisters who hunt would also cut a finger and put blood on the arrow they hunt with to share the pain with the animals and to let them know that they are sharing that moment in sacrifice to help feed their community and people. In this simple and sacred manner is the connection and symbiosis between nature and the Andean man.

The Andean man has always understood that the heart holds hope and it is important to give back what we earn to secure the future. This attitude leaves the door open for future generations of hunters in never having a lack of food for their families. With this attitude, the food is blessed. Surely there are other forms that exist on the planet in how to bless the food.

Give thanks in accepting this food that you have given us, and that our Gods have given us, like a gift to our request. This is connected to the inner knowledge, which of course already understands that these acts are very important. Every door of this connection and food should open in pairs forever and there should never be lack of food in the planet. Many are now dying of hunger. In the era of my ancestors there was always enough food. They used very simple techniques that they organized so no one would be left without food. Life is not only material but is also the love and connection towards nature as a source of life and energy.

MOTHER EARTH ITSELF OWNS

The grandfather sages understood that we humans have no right to decide for other beings on the planet. If we do, it will be we who will reincarnate as them. Therefore you do not make a decision which would affect us adversely in a next life, but do pray in a way that feeds energy to all other beings of the future.

It is important to understand that Mother Nature and the beings in her are owners of themselves and of their future. Mother Nature has a right to reclaim what is hers. We are only invited to a space for the time being. We are permitted to live in her and eat what She gives us with such kindness from a great and generous heart. She is the owner of us and we are not the owners of her.

This is a warning because since ancient civilizations, people have fought to reclaim what is not theirs; using the name of the spiritual Gods and their powers to decide and even kill their neighbors and self-proclaim states and nations with borders. They have done this despite having wide knowledge of the existence of love. Mother Nature is one and is of everybody and does not need to be divided unequally. In fact, She has her own organism that cannot be owned. Animals and plants are disappearing by the thousands in different ways because of reasons that are in our consciousness. This is happening, even though many of these beings have been here before the humans and they are the reason why we should honor one another.

It may be that animals survive for thousands of years more. But with this form of unlimited expansion, it would be very sad if our own generations should suffer from our personal whims at the moment. Every moment is precious with different energies. We know of a glacial time, which erased much of the civilization on the planet. If this were to happen again, no matter if it takes thousands of years, civilization will return. Knowing this, it is important not to squander the sacred Time given to us. We should reconcile with her and the rest of the beings and show them gratitude for the abundance that there still is. There are 7 billion inhabitants on Earth, with 8 billion projected in 2040. It is also very important not to rely entirely on machines to plant with. We should reuse the ancient ways of planting in order to have healthy food for the animals.

Animals and Mother Nature will always be guardians of the food and the safeguard of all species. We should honor her with our hearts without forgetting our own internal energy. We should plan the way that leads us to the side of spiritual wealth. That will inflate the balloon to take us to other levels.

Accepting these things leads to balance and a calm mind. The less we decide for others, the clearer our mind will be; it will not be in conflict. The truth of everything is important for us to take the next step. Feelings belong to everyone and in this case there is no room for denial. Without denial we are free.

The wise Grandfathers say that there is only one place where acceptance is found. It is in the present and now. The ancients had to be aware of what was going on all the time in order to be prepared. This knowledge was a gift for them because they understood the animals and let them fulfill the task entrusted by their Gods or fate.

But with the advent of modernity, humans have become dependent and dissatisfied with their life because their minds are not given the opportunity to naturally create. They also lack the acceptance of the truth. It is important to use the weapons of the past to see the future and in a comprehensive manner like the Andean Gods. It is also important to change denial through acceptance and commitment to oneself. Working with others is an attitude of life which will develop our personal creativity.

I want to share that in the Andean world, when a woman has 10 kilos of meat on her hands, She has to create a way to preserve the meat to feeds her children in the future. So the woman puts salt on it and lets it dry in the Sun or inside the house. This process is called Charqui. This process of dry meat can be eaten over time, spanning 5 years or more. Surely women did this to other types of food. I understand that in this way creativity is given to their lives. In the modern world if we have 10 kilos of meat, we would first refrigerate it to save it. In this way we are not giving our lives a natural form to create. The ancients were somehow independent of everything and had to solve everything using nature in a creative way.

In this way, love was created directly with the food or with other activities that took place. This is because there is a natural balance in the world that cannot always be seen, but felt. If animals continue to disappear and the birds change their direction of migration, it will be a very sad existence for man. It is important not only to live off modern living but also connect with the tools of the past to get what we should have and what we need. We are the most responsible for teaching the natural creative way to our future generations. Our ancestors could have done so with us because they had balanced and joined both ends for the happiness of everyone. It is important to know that if we give nothing in return, we will steal the natural knowledge from tomorrow that our ancestors gave to us, and that took thousands of years to assimilate. In so, we are stealing the energy required for renewal.

THE MUMMIES, INCALCULABLE SPIRITUAL VALUE

The ancient inhabitants of Peru kept their mummies in the snow so that they were preserved in time. They could then take care of the mountains and valleys because for them the mountains were alive. They were considered Apus or Gods.

To make this process of mummification, ancient civilizations first used medicinal plants for preservation. These mummies were preserved for centuries in the quarries such as Cachicata in Ollantaytambo. These mummies were discovered by grave robbers looking for riches like Incan artifacts. Even now, remains of mummification are seen exposed to the environment. But these looters do not know the real damage they caused or the sincere reason the Incas had in keeping these guardians. These guardians had sacrificed their lives to work and transport the huge monoliths of stone to the archeological ruins of Ollantaytambo. These are the buildings that still inspire and surprise us over time.

The mummies in the snow covered mountains were those who did good work in their community. They were great warriors who conquered by using multiple strategies instead of killing many people. There are also mummies of those with good qualities, such as good Fathers and Mothers. It was for this reason that the Incas did processions of their mummies in their most important festivals in their communities. They did this to show other people an example to follow. These mummies were then returned, with their mysteries, to their sacred burials in the snow covered mountains, such as in Salkantay, Ausangate and Verónica. The search of these mummies should be stopped because mummies have a priceless value in the spiritual world. They were put there for a reason with a wise connection in the spiritual levels.

To remove a stone where the mummy lays removes the charm and magic because the intention of being there is to protect us. They were buried as a gift to the mountain so that it may continue to give life to the river water that soothes thirst and feeds their children.

In the nations of the ancient civilizations, decisions about the mummies that were to be buried in the mountains were made by the wise Grandfathers and Grandmothers. Decisions about which road to take were also made, because it was a great challenge and an honor to be buried in the snow covered mountain of the regions. It is said that they took the mummies to the highest parts but first always asked permission to do so. These men wore masks and were called Ukukos. They were guardians of the mountains at the same time to ensure that nothing unnecessary happened to these gifts of great spiritual significance.

After having heard all views and aspects of the situation with regard to a certain mummy, decisions were made. This process would have taken many days but every decision was made, taking into account the wisdom that would serve the people and their destiny.

It is understood that the native communities have some simple rules for reasonable and fair decision making. The wise Grandfathers made these decisions through the wish of the community.

It is very difficult for our brothers and sisters of the Andes to rush the decision making, especially if it is about future generations, because it would affect their free development. It is a devotion, a commitment, in order for destiny to run in balance. This means that if humans understood and were willing to be accountable to make a correct decision for the lives of those born 1,000 years from now, snap decisions or wrong decisions in life that stop the free flow of energy would disappear.

The wise men that came before us understood that there is a connection that these men gave to between the Mother Earth and the Sun through the shadows of the mountains and the plants that grow. So why not make a ceremony or offering to her for her large gifts and contributions to agriculture and life and the freedom She gives us?

THE AIR, THE MESSENGER OF OUR ANCESTORS

I remember once a Grandmother of the Patacancha valleys told me that when She was a little girl She took her animals to graze. She was running through the valleys singing in the language of her ancestors with her friends. The mountains would respond to the songs using their voices in the form of the echo. These were a unique experience for her. These mountains of joy and unconditional love sing with profound sounds and guide these voices to the center and to the heart of the Earth and in circles to share with the world.

And it is there that Grandfather Air, Wayra, participates as a frequency channel to share the joy of music with the universe through the connection. They also understood that the air directs the air currents and winds through the land.

It is She that lifts the sacred birds like the Condor, the Eagle and other feathered creatures to a higher level. There, they can better see the future and life or predict many of destiny's sequences that humans miss in seeing everything personal. It is the Wind that brings the messages from our ancestors to help us rise with their good or bad experiences so that we may find the most positive aspects of a situation.

The Wind brings wisdom and kindness of the millions of years. In her silence She shares the power that gives us strength to protect everything and fills our hearts with pure wise love. This is the mystery of broad knowledge and greatness that brings the rains, and makes the thunder sing, and sends us home to take shelter and security.

We know it is an invisible being but spiritually wonderful. Perhaps we do not hear her voice on the surface, but She caresses with her whispers and encourages us to advance in the energy that we need for others. One of the beings that feels her penetration of energy is the Grandfather Tree of Life who dances to the rhythm of her teachings.

Humans need to consider that Grandfather Air is very important, as breathing is already a blessing. We should get to think that without it for a few minutes we would die and life would end forever. That is why the wise Grandfathers dedicated three coca leaves to this essential being that only brings life and in turn becomes infinite love.

THE SACRED NUMBER 3

When we walk in the mountains looking for answers to our lives, it is very important to always remember the number three; the sacred number that our ancestors used like a formula for their daily lives. Without this number their most important thought would not exist over time. So today it is known as the Inca trio of logic, which also represents the three sacred elements of the Water, the Wind and Fire in its three levels.

One of the ways we should connect ourselves with these numbers is through breathing. When we are walking through nature it is important to breathe slowly three times, as this will help us flow with the rhythm of nature in this way, securing our way to where we will go. Usually in the high Andean communities, people use the number three in their offerings to their Gods, in the best coca leaf, corn, potato or any gift that is of Mother Earth.

CONNECTING GRANDPARENTS WITH THEIR ANIMALS

The highlands of Arequipa, by Colca Canyon, which is the second deepest canyon in the world after Nepal's in the Himalayas, is where our brother and sister Condors fly to the rhythm of the Wind. They are part of the sacred Andes, where Snow caps rise to 20,000 feet or more.

In the villages of Cabanaconde and others, families can be seen living in their ancestral form. Here the Grandfathers of the communities can be seen grazing their animals. Even in their advanced age they still continue doing their chores, climbing to the tops of their Apus Gods, the mountains, and pass these animals to their children and then to their grandchildren. In this way they think in a larger picture.

The connection of the Grandfathers with their animals is very important, a practice that has been forgotten by the societies of today. To understand this we need to be living there and see the way the animals connect with their owners in an orderly manner and very special way. They jump for joy at the daily connection and responsibility to take their animals to pasture on the slopes and summits of the high Andean mountains. There, it sometimes rains but the Wind is no obstacle for them because you will always find these Grandfathers and Grandmothers in a hiding place or shelter under rocks. This is the symbiosis and love of man with their animals and nature, carrying in their shawls on their backs their cocavi or food: lima beans mixed with boiled corn and dried potatoes. They also have their herbal tea for the healing of the body, or their Chicha made of fermented corn for their thirst.

When you are in the communities sharing sacred moments with the people, they always offer a few drops of what they are drinking to Mother Earth or share it in a normal way for her to enjoy and calm her thirst. With this little detail She will help those farmers and shepherds so that their animals reproduce and that disease does not damage what they sow with so much sacrifice.

These Grandfathers could tell their everyday experience and their connection in depth with Mother Earth, or the visions they have in their eternal solitude except with their animals. Their stories would be told, despite not having gone to college or university or having been within a system. They would tell of the tools of the future and that happiness is so simple and easy to apply. So do not expect them to physically leave the Earth to the afterlife or reincarnate in silent passage on the Earth. They will have left this knowledge that is key to the period of transformation that we are living. It is related to the prophecies of 2012 which have already started, and which we can feel. It is because Father Sun is the representative of fire that is also changing. We should be prepared for these changes.

This knowledge is in each community. One example is when they cook in the ovens made of clay; they do it with the dung of animals like the llama and cattle. They do this because the smoke repels insects from eating the food (such as potatoes and meat) in their storage place on the second floor of their homes. Also the animal dung preserves the fire inside the ovens for many days - essential because these families do not have many matches available to start the fire. The fire also maintains the heat in the stone house so that the intense cold does not enter.

It is for nothing that they are still there, walking to the rhythm of the land and of the fire in the correct direction towards spiritual happiness. They do this with their characteristic simplicity so that this prophecy comes true as it is written in its beautiful and correct way.

In the total of the 7 billion people on Earth today, more that 3.5 billion people live in cities in the middle of constant noise, and with cement for their streets and paths. Rain does not naturally penetrate the cement into the soil to nurture the land, as it should be. However these waters flow through pipes to the river. This is why there is much overflow in small rivers in the villages of the valleys. But we could still learn and that is why 2012 is key for this learning of balance that we need for the great spiritual change.

Grandfather Fire is the human passion, which starts the fire in all spiritual hearts on Earth. Our inner self always teaches us to create with love using our good intentions putting our vision in practice, and keeping in each one of us the eternal flame of happiness and growth. This is increasingly strong and beautiful. Just like the Sun, you are a sacred fire which is the source of constant energy to provide solutions in the trails of life of all earthlings.

You are the Grandfather Fire that teaches to overcome with love the intentions that do not walk to the rhythm of your path. Work on reconciliation and reunification of energy to be one on Earth. In doing so, we will illuminate the sacred path of our inner and outer being in order to only see paths and love built of orchids. This keeps in the paths that teach us and allow our spirits to see the constant fire of creation for the existence of a community that belongs to everyone.

The Grandparents and Herding Communities Graze Their Animals

Ukukos, Guardians of the Mountains

Balance of love, connecting with the sunrise and sunset, with colors that are pure love and extreme beauty of nature in the eyes of their children.

Minka community work to build schools, hospitals, roads, etc..,
Because 5 fingers are more different and are united.

Lighting the sacred path of our inner and outer, to see only paths and flower orchids love built.

Offering to the snowy mountains and Mother Earth, to guide this gift into your heart and bring happiness forever.

In future generations, never lack for food in their families.

Colca Canyon, where our brothers and sisters, Condors and Grandfathers fly to the rhythm of Wind, more than 20,000 feet. Families living in an ancestral form.

Chicha, Made from Fermented Corn, Offering Thirst Split

THE ANCIENT CIVILIZATIONS ALIGNED

This very important detail of these scientific teachers of the past, forgers of all the beauties that we inherited, felt their generations would come and have difficulties with some differences between them. But they adopted a common truce with this straight line that came from the civilizations that existed in Potosi, Bolivia towards Vilca Bamba, Peru and beyond, passing other sacred places like Oruru, Tiwanaku, Amantani Island (Lake Titicaca), Pukara, Racchi the temple of Wiracocha, Cusco, Ollantaytambo, Machu Picchu and Vitcus in Vilcabamba. They lined up an incredible vision and energy between them, connecting beyond personal feelings. Each one of these holy places were ports of energy where the energy and messages were sent to the universe in antiquity and today that everything is sacred for our people.

This statement is documented and there are even more remains that are being excavated today that show that there were temples to their Gods. But how much further mystery is there or is being guarded in each one of these spaces connected with Mother Earth and her vision for her children on Earth? Time will show us the way to this greatness, breathed solely through love and happiness.

POTOSI

In Potosi, in the region of Betanzos, Province of the Department of Cornelio Saavedra of Potosi, 11 areas of Rock art have been found and registered that show a long chronology with very different representations clearly belonging to different periods. The best known, Lajas Mayu 1 (Supay Molino Khahka), shows the superimposition of different styles. This is also true at the Jatun Cueva site and at the timeline in the Lajas Mayu 2 site (Sara Cancha). You could say that the Rock art paintings are evidence of the oldest traditions of the ancestors activities in the region, apart from a set of petroglyphs which are most probably the oldest.

Early hunters produced these first manifestations, though no specific data exists to establish their date of origin at this moment.

ORURO

56 hectares with archaeological remains were found near Oruro. This place has several settlements discovered in one place. A real Tambo would have functioned in Paria, at the edge of the ravine with a full visual domain. The canyon walls are a deep red and the Wind has a little caress. Everything is flat and in solitude. Paria, "The India", is 25 kilometers from the city of Oruro and its areas are under study. It is the star of the excavations - at each step, you run into tiny fragments of pottery. It is located near the hot springs of Obrajes by Uspa-Uspa.

The Incas left a few demonstrations of real Tambos. A few were already at the site from past civilizations, and show a strategic step for the different ethnic groups that existed from thousands of years ago, including the Atawaypa. There was a high concentration of wealth here and the intent of the Incas was to regain what their ancestors of this area had planned and fulfill their intentions.

In this place, vestiges were found dating from different epochs. A llama head with fangs was found. Many call it a deity that represented a Puma Llama. Also found were representations and utensils, in stone and clay: bird shape ornothomorphic plates, stone weapons or llama and alpaca bones to make scrapers and picks, as well as many other things that are still being studied. With more work and time these may lead to the possibility of finding more tombs that will show part of the occult secrets.

TIAHUANACO

The Tiahuanaco culture was from around 1500 BC - 900 BC. It had a capitol by the same name, Tiwanaku, located on the banks of the river of the same name. The river is so beautiful and enigmatic with energy of the world of the spirits or the dead connected with life. Many Gods were worshiped by this culture. They say the Incas inherited this form of belief and wisdom because both cultures came to the threshold of wisdom and kindness towards Mother Earth and its surroundings.

This culture developed in the territories of what today are Bolivia, Chile and Peru. It expanded through their beliefs and way of work that could be seen in each of the archeological features buried in the shores of the world's highest navigable lake. Its territory started and ended at the plateau of Collao, the Chapare and up to the Pacific Ocean.

This civilization had lots of knowledge of the ecosystem and is seen today in all of the wonderful sacred ruins that the Incas inherited. The cultivation of varieties of foods that did not grow in these geographic levels is an example.

It is important to note that many of the stone monoliths that built the temple of Kalasasaya were brought from the Peruvian side about 100 kilometers away. Also note that the water level reached the shores of the temples at the era of this great civilization. With this they were able to use river transportation by boats built from totora, which could carry heavy loads up to 100 tons. They also served as transport of commercial goods and for the exchange of food.

There was a special style of ceramic pottery of the Tiahuanaco culture, which was found in Azapa, Moquegua and San Pedro Atacama. This style was also highlighted in textile art with the predominant use of alpaca, llama and vicuna fibers. They were widely technical with bronze as well as an expansion on territorial agricultural technologies such as on ridges and in terraces for cultivation.

In these temples, the general character of the trapezoidal-type gates remind us of the places built around Cusco. But for this great civilization, mythical beings in high relief can be observed in the work. One is the God of the staffs which is the most important God of this civilization. It shows four fingers on its hand, representing the four critical elements that exist: Water, Air, Fire and Earth. Its position makes it look as if it were levitating.

The ancient inhabitants of the lake knew that the lake itself was shaped like a cat or Puma. The question is: how did they know this? Is the answer that, in order to see this representation of their God, were they able to reach levels of concentration and levitation, using all of the body chakras to elevate? How is it they came to call the lake by the name of grey puma in the Aymara language? Only each one of you could answer this mystery. There are other examples like this in Peru, like the lines of Nazca from another culture, the candlestick in Paracas, or the Puma city of Cusco. I think these civilizations used many ways of realizing this: through spiritual ascension and connecting with all of the deities and beings in the universe to work together on their land, as a Mother with a son coordinating in all the decisions.

If a being is of pure spirit (i.e. morally good), then daily meditation is guided by the knowledge left by the wise ancestors for us. It is the search for enlightenment that can lead you to a direct ascension when you achieve complete knowledge, with a mind completely open and where fear and ties to this mortal world are detached.

This process usually ends with death, the point of where the being ascends. But it is also possible to ascend while alive. One may reach this state of ascending through meditation. Many beings get the same supernatural abilities including telepathy, excellent human senses, speed, strength, precognition, perfect health and healing powers.

If a natural life were our only thought, where the sounds of machines that we created do not exist, we would fly more like an Eagle or a Condor. We would need to be surrounded by direct contact with nature and its spiritual beings and respect for all. These practices were not only used in the sacred places of Tiwanaku but Wari as well, a much older civilization. Each one represented this God in Heaven. Perhaps we may even reach these ancestral levels.

AMANTANI ISLAND
This island holds many mysteries of the men who left vestiges and buildings, such as the so-called "temples" of Pachatata and Pacha Mama which are full of energy that come from sounds inside like an active volcano. Also there is the presence of extraterrestrial lights, which are seen almost daily by its inhabitants and visitors.

Arches that lead you to a greater spiritual dimension exist there, connecting to the wonderful turquoise lake, where not so cold beaches exist, despite its altitude. These arches have representative figures of their Gods and mystical beings that brought much love and energy to these islands. This is why the simplicity and smiles of the inhabitants of the villages still stand over time.

Children, women and men of Amantani and Taquile walk over its steps and cobbled paths, weaving patterns which are neither repetitive nor simple. They use their strength and greatness of their ancient culture in an effort to find the balance of love, connecting with the sunrise and sunset. These colors of pure love and extreme natural beauty astound the eyes of both the inhabitants and visitors.

They still cook with their Cconchas or kitchens made of clay and stone. They prepare aromatic plants such as muña and other plants, which provide them with a healthy spirit and body. The wrinkled faces of these inhabitants guard mysteries with wisdom that is inherited from their Grandfathers. They only share these secrets with you in the most discreet fashion. They also say that colors and flavors are in nature in an easy and instant manner.

On Amantani Island there is a place called Inca Tiana or Throne of the Inca, a place to which he came from his vast territories to rest and enjoy a day at the beach; being there they would feel the energy of the sea. The water there was warm and never cold. From here one could see the thousands of platforms of a very diversified agriculture on different peninsulas of the lake.

The beauty of Amantani and Taquile is not only the beautiful culture left behind and still continued by their heirs, but also has the beautiful flower called kantu, which is today considered the national flower of Peru. This beautiful flower complements and enhances the heat from its connection with these sacred places. It is said to brighten more with this connection.

Generally in January, the people of the island climb to the top of the hill called Pacha Mama, about 320 meters above the level of Lake Titicaca. It is about 3,810 meters above sea level. Here they sing and dance as a family and community until night falls. The ceremony is called "Payment to the Earth" in honor of Mother Earth. The Pacha Mama is given offerings for a good harvest. The wise native Paco or Shaman, chosen by the Gods, dressed in his poncho and pouch of sacred coca leaves, reads these leaves to predict the future. His colleagues, standing in circles at the ceremonial temples, help the wise Paco. To make a table or offering, the wise take various ritual objects and gifts and place them in traditional order on a cloth that is extended over the purest wool from llama or alpaca. For this ceremony they use coca leaves, llama fat, a llama fetus, incense, red wine and seashells.

It is here where the Paco greets the Gods or Apus, facing the four cardinal points. First he greets the Sun God. That is where they all lay their intentions for themselves, their family and the universe. This offering is then burned and the ash is buried in Mother Earth to send this gift into her heart and bring happiness forever.

Offerings are done facing the mountains and snow caps along the mountain range of Bolivia and Peru using a blanket of exquisite textile work. With the movement of Grandfather Wind, the sacred coca falls on the blanket and brings a message from the Gods for every being, sons and brothers on Earth. Ceremonies and activities throughout the year end the ceremony with a typical dance for each distinct God according to the clothing worn. They also make sounds using Wind instruments. They connect to the spiritual part of the mountain because for them a celebration dedicated with much satisfaction will bring spiritual greatness into the future governors of the island and to its habitants and a better harvest.

Understand that for the love of these performed rituals, this sacred place is closed 364 days a year because they want the most respect for their intention and vision. They live in each sacred space as the Gods of all sacred levels had ordered.

This is why each community and indigenous home has and prepares ceremonial tables, which they believe is as important and sacred for their future as finding small stones at different places on a pilgrimage, a practice that must be followed for the cleansing of homes and the encounter with happiness.

PUKARA

This place is so magical. It is situated on the outskirts of what once was the ancient Lake Titicaca. Upon the arrival of the Spanish, a great part of this complex pyramid and sunken temples had been destroyed. Near there, a large church has been built in an effort to change the ancestral philosophy of the town that is still based around the Pukara or the temple of Kalassaya. Stones were taken from these exquisite works for the construction of this church. Many of these stones can also be seen at the museum on site as well as the museums at the capitol of Peru, Lima.

Also at this same site, the natural Rock of the place shows the form of a cat. Could it be that the civilizations that existed before established themselves in this sacred place? It is a place where pyramids have a connection with a great port of energy that was connected with other ports of the ancient Titicaca Lake.

There is evidence that the water reached these places of Peru in the same way it reached the ports of Tiwanaku and others in Bolivia, because the energy in both places is similar. It can even be said and almost confirmed that the stones used to build Tiwanaku were brought from this part of Peru in totora boats at different times. Surely you can also feel this connection once you visit the two energy ports.

Tiwanaku and Pukara are alike for their pyramids and sunken plazas. Pukara shows proof that these knowledgeable ancient people of the truth and scientists of their natural resources carved magnificent beings, real for them but strange for us. They lived with extraterrestrial beings that used energy and their powers to move rocks to create a reality that would strike us if compared with today's technology.

Imagine Pukara surrounded by water, which made it easier to build boats of totora and to move from one place to another, not only to ship huge blocks of stone but also food and clothing to the people hit by inclement weather. It could have taken many years to build these vessels or to transport something from one place to another, but it was better than transportation through the arid mountains on this part of the continent.

This great civilization of Pukara is located 61 km north of Juliaca and on the edge of the road that leads to Cuzco. It is at 3,910 m.s.l. on the southern part of Peru in the Department of Puno, and has an area of about six square kilometers. During the years of 100 BC and 300 AD, along the shores of Lake Titicaca, the Pucara society came to the northern mountains and to the valleys of Cusco and to Tiwanaku on the south.

This civilization, in addition to having its technology of cutting and carving stones, had a very large dominance over the environment. Not only did they use what was already there, but built and invented new things. They had strange deities as Gods. These are now illegally in the hands of people who plundered hundreds of years after the Spanish arrival in the fifteenth century. Today you can still see smaller towns and villages scattered across the northern basin of Lake Titicaca.

Six constructions were found with the form of truncated pyramidal steps of ceremonial character. These demonstrate the work of these men in large numbers, commonly known as a minka in communities today. This means everyone helped build here all together all at one time. One of the most important structures is the Kalassaya pyramid of 300 m in length and 150 m wide by 30 m in height. This reflects a high concentration of labor and access to a sufficient food surplus to maintain the project. Also here is the technological knowledge for building, organizing a society, and politics to direct everything. There were many burial mounds that surely in a matter of time will open to more information about this place.

This civilization had a notable expansion, 500 kilometers to the west of the lake and many dozens of kilometers on the east side. Also they are known for their buffer or bridge between the Chavin and Tiwanaku civilizations. They dominated in agriculture as well as in the rearing of animals in high altitudes and the combined work of men and women to achieve the balance in their societies.

Doing agriculture in terrains of flooding along the shores of Lake Titicaca, they assured cultivation for an intensive altitude with a diet based on potato, olluco, oca, mashua, and corn, the latter to a lesser proportion compared to the production in the regions of Suni and Puna. There were many irrigation canals for their terraces and they traded with the different people of all the valleys to obtain different goods.

Today when you go by these highland valleys you see many of the inhabitants, raising hundreds to thousands of llamas and alpacas. These animals serve as a means of transportation of cargo between all activities of exchange. In the water were the totora but in the valleys and mountains the llamas and alpacas were used. Also, in excavations there are many quantities of these mature animals. It just shows that the Pukcaras domesticated these animals for the same reason we see today; these animals could carry cargo from 15 to 75 kg depending on their size.

The Andean man's coexistence with these animals is impressive because both the alpaca and the llama were animals of real value. The llama is a type of artiodactyls mammal of the Camelidea family. It is a great animal native to the Andes, which was domesticated in southern Peru. In all of these places people used it in respectful offerings to Mother Earth for her contributions. Remains have been found at a height of 3,800 meters or more.

Their contributions to the ancient societies as the Pucaras and today's society are as follows:
Their wool for textiles of wool blankets and much more.

The dry nails as a musical instrument.

Their leather to sleep on and to make footwear.

Their bones for musical instruments such as the quenas (Andean flute)

The bones as tools for weaving.

The flesh as food or dried in the Sun or shade with salt for later consumption.

As a pack animal to carry seeds and other items of agriculture to high altitudes.

The dried dung as fuel for cooking and as a fertilizer for plants.

Its fat boiled in pots and then mixed with clay and straw in the coatings that served to waterproof constructions. To this day buildings have been protected and conserved with this mixture, despite heavy rainfalls.

It is also said that the llama brought in armies to conquer villages near the jungle. The llama was first sent and they guided everyone else towards water or the correct path.

The llama was raised intensively during the Pre-Hispanic era as the only cargo animal. There existed enormous herds of cargo llamas to transport products and there was even a special race, much bigger and stronger, for these purposes. Today, this breed is very rare. Llama meat was eaten fresh or sun-dried for storage in the form of jerky.

Huge reserves of jerky existed in warehouses, or colcas,. Llama fiber was used to make textiles, ponchos, tapestries and other garments. Leather ropes and strong tie straps were also made of llama.

The Pukaras were also great and technically savvy potters with impressive techniques of ceramics to create such art as tall bowls with annular bases. They had a reddish color surface and were decorated with black, grey and yellow colors. With the presence of the lake in the form of a feline and the Rock in Pukara of the same shape, they created pottery designs of cats, fish, llamas and well-crafted musical instruments.

The Pukara ancestors were great stonecutters and surpassed other civilizations like Chavin de Huantar, in lytic cutting forms, polishing and the binding of rocks and columns.

RACCHI
Racchi has one of the most beautiful buildings which combines giant adobe with stones in a cell type construction. The most important building in the complex is the "Temple of Wiraqocha", which according to old chroniclers, was built by the Inca Wiraqocha in tribute to the superior invisible Gods of the Andean people. The Apu Kon Titi Wiraqocha structure is large enough to gather 1,000 people or more. It has a trapezoidal shape and windows decorated with chacanas painted in red. But with

the erosion of time and neglect about 80% of the structure has been erased.

This place was called the Temple of Wiracocha, the God and creator of the universe, who teaches man to cultivate and harvest their land with knowledge and tools that are still in use today. They also taught the planning of their homes in positioning them to the sunrise of June 21st and December 22nd, related to the most important days for these past civilizations, the days of Harvest and Sowing.

In Racchi you can see huge barns where food for families was kept in case of a bad harvest, and which they had access to so no one would be deprived of food. These constructions in circular forms were called Machu Qolqas, which preserved food. These old barns were where these men first began with the first well planned giant barns. Here, the leader of 1 family, 10 families, 100 families, 1,000 families, etc., was responsible for receiving taxes and getting food to these places called tambos. There it was kept for later distribution to the different villages.

This great temple of initiation oversees the wide roads that lead to different directions and sacred places, like Cusco and Lake Titicaca. Here you can see how the stone was laid to make the roads last over time. Humidity was not an obstacle even as millions of people passed over them.

You can see the walls that covered this wonderful place that hold many mysteries. On the top of the mountain one can observe remnants of three volcanoes called by the locals "Kinsach'ata." They worshipped them and still make offerings to this day. The people can still feel their energy and work the land in their ancestral way. You can see this in the natural beauty of the place.

Here, there is a small lake with many fine ceramics around it. They come from towns that were dedicated to the development of pottery in quantity. Surely these tools and ornaments of clay are also stored in those circular barns. These potteries also used to transport some products with ropes of straw, sheep's wool and sticks, which were tied to llamas and alpacas to make transportation easier. There were also fine potteries, which made objects of offerings for the various sacred sites.

This small lake is home to many migratory birds. The ceremonial springs of standing water in their surroundings look like giant mirrors, which make this place even more mysterious and enigmatic. This water that comes from the volcanoes was used for purification. It is important to touch the water, taste it and feel the sacred vital fluid. If it is sufficiently strong in the stomach, Mother Earth would know and would purify it in a crystalline way throughout the year. This is done as it flows through the channels that have run for thousands of years, feeding this small lake with so much natural beauty.

Most surprising is that the descendants of men and women who built Racchi still work on the terraces and fields of crops that their ancestors left. Here, the colorful haba flowers can be seen. The tarwi and the corn and potatoes grown here enhance the area and restore it as it was thousands of years ago. Their connection with Mother Earth is so special that all they do is smile and it permeates the heart of every one of us that transit through the area. It makes us think that the intention of the civilization is so beautiful that they did not want to transform the land but use it to live, not just survive.

There is a small community near the temple of Wiracocha which is still called Raqchi. It belongs to the district of San Pedro de Cacha in the province of Canchis. Raqchi is on the right bank of the Willca Mayu River in Vilcanota at an altitude of 3,500 m.s.l (11,500 feet.) A complex town of multiple buildings, Raqchi includes terraces inclined at 5 degrees up the hills for cultivation and for various purposes, like kanchas, "wayranas" qolqa barns. It was possibly also used as a tambo or resting place on the road to "Collasuyo". The Grandfathers of the town say that this town was built because there was a man in the ancient civilization that posed supernatural powers. He taught all the inhabitants the ways and times for planting and harvesting, and also performed miraculous healings.

Pedro Cieza de Leon collected the tradition that said that the temple was built after the appearance of a man who performed miracles in this place. This makes me think of the theory of Jesus Christ, who may have been in these places. This man had a beard and looked different to the others. This story was not lost but kept hidden from communication. The Grandfathers of the place know and it is in their hearts and minds what really existed and who had been here. The only thing now is to rediscover it and bring it out to share with others.

Pedro Cieza de Leon says that the villagers had decided to stone him. But in going after him they found him on his knees with his arms extended and a rain of fire immediately fell. Thus these sorry men let him go and this strange man had gone to the coast and plunged into the waters of the ocean and disappeared forever. After this a temple was built in his memory and an idol was sculpted out of stone. According to some of the Spaniard conquistadors who saw it, said the idol was the image of a Christian apostle that passed through these lands. Calling the rain of fire may be referred to as an eruption of the "Kinsach'ata" volcano that is not currently active. Around the area there are a lot of dry lava and volcanic stones.

The "Temple of Wiraqocha" is a grandiose construction for its era. Architecturally it is classified as "kallanka" i.e. a large building completely covered with straw (wood and "ichu"). On the outside it measured 92 m (302 feet) long by 25.25 m (83 feet) wide. Its central wall was made with finely carved stones, its base has a height of about 3 m of adobe, its walls have 1.65 m of thickness at the base and about 1.30 m on top. Today this wall is 12 m tall but its original height was 15 m or possibly 16.60 m. Its side walls were1.20 m thick and 3 m in height.

The roof was impressive with almost 2,500 m and an inclination of about 50 degrees. There were round columns that are still found at the base near the central wall and the sidewall to support the thatched roof made of clay mixed with the fat of llama. The columns were 1.60 m in diameter and about 9.80 in height.

CUSCO
In the Runa Simi language, Quechua, our ancestors called it Qasqo, which means chest or navel, and so the Mother of the Inca civilization is known as the navel of the world. At an altitude of 3,400 meters above sea level, this extraordinary city was built in the shape of a Puma, which can only be observed from the higher parts of the mountains or in a plane. Unfortunatley, its shape has been destroyed with the passage of time and the growth of city.

A grandfather of the surrounding communities told me that it was there where many of our ancestors and sacred animals of those times came to rest in peace. Cusco may also have been that place in the next step for the afterlife, like finding answers for the next reincarnation. For this reason it is understood now that many of the buildings in this magnificent place have carvings in forms of Snakes, Pumas and Condors on their walls and doors.

The Grandfathers say that the Condor is the messenger of the Gods. It takes the spirit of the dead towards the spiritual world where the Sun and the Wirachocha, God of creation, will pass justice over the person. Also, the Condor was the union of the present world with the world of the spirits; the serpent was the connection of the present world with the world of the dead and the physical; and so the puma maintained the balance and guided all beings with his audacity and power.

There is a story to tell of when I was a child in Ollantaytambo. On occasion I would see the condors that would fly over the sacred areas in circles. Then I heard that a condor was found on the banks of the sacred river Willca Mayu. I thought about a story told by my grandfather. The presence of this majestic bird was to be purified with the sacred waters, which river represents the Milky Way. Its spirit would return to her (Milky Way) and then later return to find its sacred place in the valley of Cusco, to rest and enter another spiritual level.

For healers and teachers who verify this version, they say that they know these birds and animals who feel a special connection with the Grandfathers of different civilizations that lived here, spirits which telepathically invited sacred animals and other beings. So, like the Condor, they would fly in circles and be part of the various sacred ceremonies.

Cusco is surrounded by giant and majestic archaeological sites and temples, which are known as: Saqsayhuaman, Qenqo, Tambo Machay and many others. They are being studied and still guard wonderful energy in connection with the heart and mind of Mother Earth within them. Inside, there are tunnels or mysterious three-dimensional doors that lead to different sacred parts of this wonderful city, which actually was more beautiful than the present city of Machu Picchu. But with the arrogance and greed of the invaders, this city was destroyed on the same land where ancient civilizations had built and lived in and kept building until the arrival of these men of the West.

When you are in Saqsayhuaman you will understand the infinite love of these men and women of the past towards their societies. Their infinite love towards their children and heirs who would inhabit these places for thousands of years to come is apparent. In these times, we are amazed by the work of thousands of years which were subject by civilization after civilization as they dominated mental powers in all dimensions and directions. We do not understand how the first inhabitants of this place communicated with those that came after to have them continue the work started, so that they endure over time with dedication and hard work and with a vision of the future.

On the walls of Saqsayhuaman, there are whimsical animal forms which were jealous guardians of the city. Today, despite the destruction suffered, they keep the numbers of stone walls of untold determination of will that only a heart and mind in unity might be able to construct.

Qenqo has labyrinths in which numerous remains of pottery and stone artifacts which were used for ceremonies have been found. Also found were objects of bone, which could explain that this place was used to mummify the bodies of those men who were to be positioned in the mountains and glaciers for their conservation and as guardians of the mysteries.

When you touch the flat stone inside the labyrinths of Qenqo, the temperature is always cold, despite the intense heat of the surroundings. This cold temperature helped preserve the mummies. Blood and water of herbs, like Molle, were used in mummification. These were taken as offerings to the snake shaped channels found in the top of the Rock of Qenqo, next to the carved forms of pumas, condors, etc.

These canals also guided these liquids to the depths of Mother Earth for her awakening with joy and to give these people an abundance of food and good weather. Bumps can also be observed. When they create shadows, they show the exact dates for these ceremonial activities and mummification.

Tambo Machay is a temple dedicated to water, which comes from a spring that has run for thousands of years with pure and healthy water. These men and women built fountains to represent the duality of black and white, woman and man, etc. Here also was built beautiful carved stonewalls representing forms of birds and the hands of ancient warriors.

Tambo Machay was visited by many rulers of the past to rest and drink its water after their hard work at each of their towns. They did so because it was impossible to poison the water here as it comes from a spring. 70% of the most important archaeological ruins that exist receive water from springs. Cusco and its most important temples, such as the Temple of the Sun, Cori Cancha, used water from springs and were also built in the highest parts of the ancient wet valley of Cusco. It is said that here is the presence of subsoil water, as well as the presence of an ancient lake, which is the remnant of the lake now called Huacarpay.

In the construction of the ancient city of Cusco, different colors of granite were used, which contained a percentage of quartz. This is similar to the one seen at the palace of the Inca Roca, where the stone of 12 angles is shown. This perhaps was the representation of a map of the Incas, the representation of the twelve sides of the Andean cross, or was simply a keystone. It is a mystery of where and how they brought the thousands and millions of stones to Cusco as a whole. Its construction was done at different times. Only you can find the satisfaction of knowing the truth in your spiritual response. These stones are those that keep many mysteries and secrets and at the same time each one of these stones holds healing properties in some way. It is the only material thing that will survive over time. The noise of cars and commercialism of the streets may bother you at times, but there are many mysteries that you should find out about. Even if you live in a hotel downtown you will discover incredibly constructed walls as you walk through the different streets and sidewalks.

This city in the southeastern part of Peru is located in the eastern slopes of the Andes, at the Hautanay River Basin, tributary of Vilcanota. It is stated in the Peruvian Constitution as the country's historic capital. Cusco was also the capitol in the ancient Inca civilization. It now has a population of about 500,000 people according to the latest census, of which there are migrants who come from nearby valleys to improve their economic development.

Pedro Cieza de León. Chronicle of Peru, 1553
The night illumination of the city is of original form, as it was found at the time of the conquest of the Inca Empire. Cuzco was of the same name as in current Quechua, Qusqu or qosqo. It is estimated that the name had an Aimariaco origin, of the phrase qusqu wanka (Rock of the Owl) from the story of the brothers Ayar. Ayar Auca occupies the site of Cuzco flying with his own wings to perch on a Rock in the area and become a brand of occupation:

"Go fly there (as they said he was born with wings), and sitting there take position on the same spot where the landmark appears, because we will go later to settle and live." Ayur Auca, hearing the words of his brother, flew over his brother and went to that place which Manco Capac sent him. Sitting there, he was turned into stone and became the landmark, which in the ancient language of this valley is called a cozco, from where the name stayed as Cuzco until this day.

Juan Diez de Betanzos says the etymology of the name has been lost in popular knowledge, and has been obscured. Betanzos himself cites:

Of which people called the inhabitants thereof, from its antiquity, Cuzco, and what this meaning of the name Cozco is, they do not know, even as it was so called in ancient times. The first chroniclers noted the name of the city almost invariably as Cuzco or Cozco by a few, as in the spelling in the sixteen-century Spanish was in the process of readjustment of the sibilant consonants, best was a closer sound of Qusqu [_qo_s.qo].

A totally different etymology was proposed by the Inca Garcilaso de la Vega Chimpu Ocllo, who says they had put as a spot or center of the Tawantinsuyo the city of Cozco, in which in the particular language of the Incas means the heart or navel of the Earth or world.

Looking at the map of what was Cuzco at the time of the Incas, you can see the shape of a cat. Two Inca legends attribute its foundation to it first head of state, the legendary Manco Capac, with his consort Mama Ocllo. In both it is stated that the place was revealed by the Sun God (Inti) to its founders after a pilgrimage that started south of the Sacred Valley of the Incas. The Father Sun had entrusted a golden spike and told them that where this sinks, there the city of the Gods will be founded.

It is said that because of the imminent migration to other towns of Tiwanaku, they decided to go to the valleys of Cuzco, as this showed them a wealth of riches. Note that there were many people already living with a vast knowledge of agriculture and other activities of life. 500 men of Tiwanaku gradually established themselves in the valley of the Hautanay River, a process that culminated with the founding of Cuzco. The approximate date is unknown, but according to traces found, it is agreed that where the city is located it has been inhabited for 3,000 years or more. However, it was considered as the capitol of the Inca civilization of the thirteenth century and also considered as the oldest inhabited city in the Americas.

It is worth mentioning that this valley was inhabited by many ethnic groups which already had inherited knowledge from their ancestors. The Guallas, the Sahuasiray, and the Antasayas are noted as the oldest inhabitants, while the Alcavizas, the Copalimaytas and Culunchimas are considered as the most recent. It is also known that the Ayarmacas inhabited the region, being the only ones not bowing to the Incas and becoming their main rival in the dominion of the counties.

The ruler Pachacutec restored Cuzco as the spiritual and political center. Pachacutec came to power in 1438. He and his son, Tupac Yupanqui, devoted five decades to the organization and reconciliation of the different tribal groups under their control, including Lupaca and Colla. That is where the North was reached to what is now Quito, Ecuador and the Maule River in Chile to the South. He culturally integrated the inhabitants of 4,500 km of mountain ranges.

The civil war between the two brothers, Huascar (Golden Chain) and Atahualpa (Brave Warrior), both born from two princesses of different regions and of the Tawantinsuyo were also sons of Huayna Ccapac. Thanks to this error of having two sons, the two royal princesses had to leave their power to each of their sons, Huascar and Atahualpa.

Huayna Capac said to Atahualpa, that, as you were born in Quito, Ecuador, I leave you this place as a capitol and you can conquer more to the North. Use the arrows made out of chonta wood, a material that is very close to here and is at your fingertips.

Huascar was also told that, you were born in Cusco, I leave you this city as a capitol, which is conquered and expanded and with unified villages. Your goal is to conquer the jungle with Huaraca (flying ball weapons), spears and clubs.

But before his Father died, Atahualpa became very unsatisfied because he saw that all the riches were already in Cusco. He decided to invade his brother with force. He killed him, using the arrows that were still unknown in these parts of the Tawantinsuyo.

Atahualpa did not live in Cusco, but lived in Cajamarca. This is another department in today's Peru. The people of Cusco were dissatisfied by his daring murder of his brother and being taken over by force. Today there are still plenty of traces of his presence in Cajamarca, such as fountains, agricultural areas and other landmarks.

This is precisely when the Spanish arrived. The Cuzquenians at this time lent their support in the battle to beat Atahualpa, not knowing the real intention that these white men had. So that is how the inhabitants of these valleys of Cusco were confused and how they thought the Spanish came to help free their people from the hands of Atahualpa. In the past there was also a white man with a beard who lived with them and was very good.

It is also important to note that for the release of Atahualpa, it was ordered to fill large rooms with gold and silver to the height of where his fingers reached. The Spanish came to see that much gold and silver was brought and began to pull some away from the room. Atahualpa was unable to fill the rooms as he promised, so he was sacrificed and died. He was charged of a reality that these white men did not know: the fall of the Inca civilization and the destruction of many legacies and structures to build palaces and churches that are seen in each indigenous town today.

OLLANTAYTAMBO

Located in the Sacred Valley of the Incas, it is the most important axis between Cusco and the edge of the jungle, Machu Picchu. This is where they exchanged many products such as corn for the coca leaf or potatoes for fruits. It is also a very important energy port because after Cusco, Ollantaytambo was built with over 600 hectares including temples, terraces, fountains, centralized towns, etc.

Ollantaytambo was the second most important sacred space after Cusco for its location being in the middle of three valleys and also the presence of communities, which still jealously guard the philosophy and tools of our ancestors, as if time had not passed. These practices continue in the minds and hearts of every citizen in the communities.

In many of the 36 communities currently in Ollantaytambo, 100% of the population speak Quechua, the language of their ancestors. The language is taught to young children, and spoken when playing or in town meetings. It is understood how this language is romantic and strong at the same time. I want to mention that some of the communities still keep these instruments they call happiness, essential to their existence, which in practice are not very complicated, but help to easily understand many things of everyday life. In the Patacancha basin the communities are called Yanamayu (black river), Qelqanqa (writings or drawings), Waca Wasi (House of livestock), Patacancha (high village), and Willoc. These are the most indigenous communities and it is important to visit them.

In these communities, Grandfathers and Grandmothers are still found following their traditions of true shamans and sages, ancestors who saw the future of these societies in a very interesting way through the constant use of the sacred coca leaf, by ceremonies and offerings to the land with the community.

It is also important to note when traveling, to observe all the women and men of the basin working together, for example in the construction of community halls, schools, medical clinics and many other projects, as in the past.

Ayni or the Minka is still the way of working and it is practiced among women and men of the communities. The Ayni is community work done with a great sense of solidarity and performed by eligible members and on behalf of each Ayllu. This work is carried out for agricultural purposes or for an urban sense (building houses). This example of joint work can be seen visiting the villages surrounding the town of Ollantaytambo, where it is possible to see the inhabitants go to different places to provide the Ayni with their neighbors in preparing or harvesting their land or working together to build a house. This practice is taught to their children and they become accustomed to it. This kind of practice is important to use at all times and must be kept in the future, as it is important to keep these little traditions for the balance of the universe.

Following the creek of Patacancha in Ollantaytambo one can see a large amount of Inca agricultural terraces still in use and many of them still maintain their aqueducts. Around two hours of hiking along the creek is the Pumamarka (The People of the Puma), which was a strategically important town in Inca times and is at an altitude of 3,600 m.s.l.

In the canyon called Pachar there are many sacred remains such as the Ñaupa Church. It is very impressive to see for its well-carved stones, carved as if by laser. Civilizations later built terraces and rooms of worship and care. According to local Shamans, these later cultures understood that these were places of energies and of concentration, which should be used as a source of pure energy.

Continuing down the Pachar canyon there are white Rock art, since there already exist rocks of this color. Probably blending the juices of native plants, these were painted to express feelings of that time, focused on their connection and inspiration. Painting is an art of all times by men and women, showing man as a being, since its origin on Earth, capable of performing works of art on the walls of the caves he inhabited. In addition to Rock art on boulders, there were sculptures, decorated ceramics and ornamental objects.

The paintings on the walls of caves, in which humans and animals are represented, can be found in every part of this canyon, in Cusco, as well as on all the continents of Earth. It seems that all human groups throughout the stages of life, time and space created this type of profound and lasting work in expressing the special spiritual relationship with other beings and creatures of their environment and with their Gods. The motives and materials of the different Rock art of the canyon bear a resemblance with those found thousands of miles away and thousands of years apart.

In Pachar Canyon, there are small villages called Soqma, Pillco Bamba, Rayan and Marcuray, which are also descendants of our ancestors. They still live there despite that their children have to walk many miles to reach their different study centers, sometimes up to 2 hours there and two hours back. It may be that the wonder of working on cultivating the Earth and the connection with each of their animals rewards this effort.

In these villages there are many mysteries yet to be solved because the work done using two cattle or sometimes two strong men to plow the land surprises everyone. It is especially true for visitors who in their societies are more interested in the machine and forget that there still exists a connection in ancestral forms of working the land.

I once had the opportunity to go to the village of Pillco Bamba and one of the town people named Mario Coyso arrived to my tent at midnight. I woke up and the moon was very bright and you could see the Milky Way with the Andean Cross. I then asked Mario where he was going and he told me he was going to cut and gather plants that served as foliage for his animals. He also told me that the Mother Moon and the stars feed the plants and have a relationship with agriculture so we must worship her when She is present. While we are working, She enlightens us with her love and her beauty. He then said that this is where we are inspired and become again beings of the night in order to move ahead and as we try to send our prayers to our deities.

In Pilco Bamba, there is the presence of a waterfall called Perolniyoc, which is a source of inspiration and connection with the water. It is medicine for the soul and the diseases that want to eradicate the body. Closer to the waterfall, the vibration is much stronger which makes you breathe in a way that reaches the depths of your being and transforms you into a new being of the water with enough energy to climb a mountain with the protection of this sacred water.

The purifying waters of this place reflect in your face. This being of life knows your feelings and virtues, as a son of the land to which power will grow. To know the feelings of others as She knows yours will connect you and help you understand as they do. These spirits of the sacred water always sing the songs of the rivers and seas in which they flow into, renewing the tears of beings just as they renew the lives of many generations.

The sacred waters of the Perolniyoc take all aspects that are born pure in the summits of the mountains of the place, just like the dew of plants and flowers that fall drop by drop to reach their destination and fulfill their mission to renew the life of the many messenger beings.

Sacred is the water because you dance to the rhythm of the thunder and announce your arrival of your tears to smother the thirst of the desert. In this way with your partners, the humans, you work the land to make energy grow - that is the food for your children. But the best products you take to honor and speak to the major Gods that it is something very just and necessary in the offering they make. For that reason, we should now stop the famine that is threatening modern societies. Every 5 seconds a child less than 10 years old dies for the lack of food in Latin America, something that in ancient societies never happened.

But the most surprising thing of you, water of the Perol Niyoc, is that you come from the clouds. You pass by streams and through the rivers, flow into the ocean, but your love for the beings makes you return to the clouds to sacrifice yourself once again to feed the billions of beings. This is regardless of their indifference to save you, respect and stop further contamination that forms a barrier against your free development.

You are a sacred depository of Mother Earth, where we learn from you for your love and freedom to become organized and to follow the flow of energy and to share it with others as you share it with us, your brothers. You make us understand that it is important to follow the flow with which we were created by our Gods. And to stop the disturbance and the obscure from our real growth without any distractions and fear of going along to the next level you already know and return from, for the love of your brothers in their organic and emotional growth.

But even more surprising is that our Grandfathers and Grandmothers built Cori Marca in a well positioned place where we can see Northern Eagles and Southern Condors through the Perolniyoc valleys, which are connected with an endless amount of constructions throughout the sacred valley, with canals made for the flow of water and the nourishment for all beings along its way.

Ollantaytambo is located in the Urubamba province, with 36 communities and sectors, and has a population of about 13,000 inhabitants. It is at an altitude of 2,792 m.s.l. It once had a plaza named Manyaraqui.

During the Inca Empire, Pachacútec conquered the region and built the town and a ceremonial center. At the time of the conquest it served as a fort for Manco Inca Yupanqui, leader of the Inca resistance, in which two battles were fought. In the first, the Incas won by flooding the river so the Spanish horses could not cross it. They later returned with more men where Manco Inca Yupanqui had to abandon and retreat to Vilcabamba but not through Machu Picchu. In fact he used another more secure and wider path between Ollantaytambo and Vilcabamba (the Amaybamba Valley). He made the route through the Picchu gorge, which was used least. He understood they would be followed and so he took another shortcut through Malaga to reach his goal of Vilcabamba, when the Spaniards later arrived.

The shortcut guided the Spanish through another route and thus they never got to know this great sacred space called Machu Picchu, saving it from the building of Spanish churches and cathedrals on top of its beautiful Incan buildings.

Ollantaytambo is the only city of the Incas still inhabited in Peru. There are terraces of resistance (to prevent the erosion of the mountain). If you would unearth a layer you would find a layer of Earth over a layer of clay for the sole purpose of Agriculture. The clay acts to keep the soil moist, so it is not necessary to water all the time. This helps decrease the sliding of the terraces.

The village of Ollantaytambo, with its straight, narrow and quaint streets today contains fifteen city blocks located north of the city's main square. This, in itself, is a true historical legacy. It is impressive, as a city plan is still inhabited today, where gardens for medicinal plants and herbs, animals and waterways that lead water to each family still exist. There is an impressive organization. Even more important is knowing that our ancestors lived all together in one place, regardless of their economic level or social class. This made it easier for the ruler to bring water or other resources to one place.

Ollantaytambo is located on both banks of the Patacancha River, close to the point where it joins the Willcamayu River, now known as the Urubamba River. Here, huge food storages or barns are seen on the tops of the mountains, as they also served as tambos or inns, resting places for dominating from the high mountains, a large part of the valley. This is one of the most monumental architectural complexes in civilization, due to its massive walls.

. Stones were brought from quarries 7 km up and down the valley. This makes Ollantaytambo one of the most unique and amazing artworks made by ancient men and women. Especially impressive is the Temple of the Sun and its giant monoliths of pink granite and red porphyry.

According to some scholars and historians, the architectural complex of Ollantaytambo belongs to the Inca Empire era, in-between the Pachacútec and Wayna Capac Incas. This stage was comprised by only three generations of Inca rulers and that preceded the conquerors by only 150 to 200 years. The apparent small amount of time that existed between design and construction of this granite citadel or fortress, have many researchers in doubt regarding its true origin.

Ollantaytambo stores among many things, the secret of two legends: The Tunupa and the General Ollanta. In the first, it speaks of a messenger of the Gods who came to town long before the creation of the Inca Empire, dressed as a beggar and seemed to be very old. Upon arrival he was welcomed by the inhabitants of the place, especially by their Curaca or Chief who received him with all honors. Thankful for this, Tunupa gave up the staff with which he traveled. Legend has it that at the birth of the son of the Curaca, the staff turned into gold. The eldest son was called Manco Capac., He left Ollantaytambo taking it in his hands and later plunged it into a nearby mountain in Cusco. The Huanacauri then decided to establish the Inca Empire and create there its capitol or most important city.

OLLANTA AND CUSI COYLLUR
The second talks about a young man called Ollanta, who was born in a tambo about 700 years ago. Tambos were places where large amounts of food were stored and scattered throughout the valleys at certain amounts of kilometers in distance so that the Inca Army or other people of the government or society could have access to it as lodges and which included meals.

This certain tambo was between Machu Picchu and Cusco in the sacred valley. The story goes that Ollanta was a very intelligent child who was born of a lower class people, but he held a very special natural gift. It is said that he dreamt that one day he would be chosen to do lots of work in his community. As all inhabitants, he wanted to enlist in the army and from there serve the Inca in their desire to further expand the empire. Ollanta did not understand why he had so many special natural gifts and creativity but knew that being always active, creativity would come to him.

At the age of 18 he decided to join the Inca's army. At that time, the entire empire was ruled by the Inca Pachacutec (restorer of the world), who was the material God. Realizing the gifts of this young man, he asked him if he wanted to be general of a battalion in his army. And so from that moment, Ollanta could enter the Inca's palace - something an army soldier could not do.

They say that Ollanta, upon entering the palace for the first time, saw the daughter of the Inca Pachacutec. Her name was Cusi Coyllur (Star or Joyous Light).They fell in love at first sight. However, this love was kept in secret, because the daughter of the Inca could only marry another Inca and not one of its people. That was not acceptable.

The Inca did not know of his daughter's romance with this man of the lower class. It is said that it was kept in secret over a long time and that a friend called Piki Chaqui (Flea Feet), server to the Inca, was who connected them and knew everything that happened between the young couple.

The drama continues when the Inca Pachacutec faced serious problems in a given territory. In concern, he sent Ollanta to defend the territory from attacks by the enemies. But before he left the Inca said: "If you win and bring victory, then you could ask for whatever you like and I will give it to you." Ollanta was excited at the thought that by winning, he could ask for the hand of Cusi Coyllur. He then turned to face the enemy and in a strong battle against the Chancas, was victorious. Meanwhile, in the palace, the Inca Pachacutec had discovered that his daughter was expecting a child in her womb.

The Inca, hearing of this sent to lock the princess in an Aclla Huasi, the house of the Inca chosen women, for betraying the Inca customs. At that time, Ollanta returned from the war triumphant and dreamed that at last he could marry the daughter of the Inca. Thus, on returning to Cusco, he was received by the Inca who asked him what his request was for defeating their enemies. Then, Ollanta said, "Honorable Inca, all I desire in my life for defeating the enemy is to be able to marry Cusi Collur, as She is expectant with my child. I know it is against the law and customs that we have, but the Gods will forgive what all this has caused, because our love is beyond the boundaries of our belief.

The Inca became both sad and bitter and only said, "Ollanta, get out of my palace before I kill you." He felt betrayed by his general and his daughter. Ollanta, angry and frustrated, left for his tambo and began to assemble his own army to defeat the Inca for the princess's hand. Before long, Ollanta had already prepared a strong army to fight for the hand of Cusi Coyllur or to at least rescue her. He could not have his daughter be born there and was said to be the new morning star and of inner beauty. And so he named her Ima Sumaq meaning "Inner Beauty".

But before going to war for the rescue of his beloved, two generals appeared. They were supposedly friends of Ollanta, and entered through the two gates to the town of Ollantaytambo. The two said that the Inca had thrown them out of Cusco and no longer wanted them. They looked tired with torn clothes and blood on their faces, but it all was a trap devised by the Inca as he suspected that the power of this General Ollanta grew more and more.

The two generals misled him by saying they wanted to join him to help regain his love from the enclosure in which this evil Inca had put her. Ollanta, on hearing this, was pleased. He ordered the whole town to celebrate because two friends had come to help him achieve his purpose of recovering his beloved and daughter. They all drank plenty of corn Chicha and were drunk. Thus, these two traitors, seeing that everyone was in critical condition, opened the two main entry doors to Ollantaytambo. The Inca army came in and took Ollanta prisoner to Cusco.

When they reached the imperial city they were surprised to learn that the Inca Pachacutec was feeling unwell and had to leave the palace and power to his eldest son Inca Tupac Yupanqui, the eldest brother of Cusi Coyllur. On seeing Ollanta, Tupac Yupanqui was surprised in seeing a strong man before his eyes. Then, Mother Nature (Pacha Mama) said: "Forgive this man because he will give you many victories and help you expand your empire beyond what you can imagine." On sensing this message, Tupac Yupanqui stared at Ollanta and saw the beauty of the light that surrounded this man and became scared and said: "Ollanta, I know my Father did wrong on sending you away. I forgive you, but first I wonder if you want to marry my sister." Ollanta replied, "That is my future and I cannot live without them. My heart feels empty and cries, even as a warrior. But Mother Earth comforts me and tells me that the son of this Inca will forgive you as we have given you this light that protects you."

Then the prince said: "Before you marry my sister you will have to build the Temple of the Sun in Ollantaytambo and a bridge that will connect Ollantaytambo with other tambos." Ollanta was pleased, gladly accepted, and began building the Temple of the Sun and the Inca Bridge. And as in every story, Ollanta married the daughter of the king, Cusi Coyllur, and had next to him his daughter, Ima Sumaq, and they were happy and ate partridges.

But before finishing this story, I will tell you that when Ollanta died, Mother Earth put his body on a sacred mountain in Ollantaytambo to inspire future generations and one day rise again to show an example of this great culture. This formation can be seen from the ruins, from afar, sleeping with his hands on his abdomen and his face towards the heavens in thanks to his Father the Sun, his God, for the happiness that he gave and for his victories.

This drama is very important, because it is still present in the minds of many relatively old people in the village of Ollantaytambo and their communities. It is they who told of the Inca shape in the mountains where large ruins are found of terraces and temples, as well as urban areas like Choquebamba and others that enjoy the admiration of the farmers of the valley.

In Ollantaytambo there is a lost village that is at the back of the ceremonial fountains, on arable lands, where it just happens that Marcaccocha lagoon is, in the Patacancha basin. So when this civilization lived in this lower part of what is today called the sacred area or the temples, this lagoon overflowed and brought with it mud that buried the town. Digging is being done gradually and you can notice these buildings and you cannot say it necessarily belonged to the Incas but a Pre-Inca culture. For that reason the Incas moved to the highest parts such as the current Inca town of Ollantaytambo.

MACHU PICCHU

Machu Picchu is a very spiritual place where all the magic is combined. This part is attributed to the rediscovering of Machu Picchu by Hiram Bingham who arrived in Machu Picchu in 1911. The first direct references to visitors to the ruins of Machu Picchu indicate that Augustine Lizarraga, a lessee of land in Cusco, arrived at the sacred site on July 14, 1902 accompanied by Gabino Sanchez, Enrique Palma and Justo Ochoa.

They left a marker with their name on one of the walls on the Temple of the Three windows, which was subsequently verified by several people. There is Information that Lizarraga had visited Machu Picchu in the company of Lius Bejar in 1894, showing portions of buildings to his companions, but at that time there were no investigations as to who built them or for what activities they were built.

Hiram Bingham, an American history professor, was interested in finding the last Inca redoubts of Vilcabamba, in which he had heard of Lizarraga from his contacts with local landowners. It was they who led him to this mysterious place, as well as Pablo Recharte, a youth of about 11 years, son of a peasant who already lived in Machu Picchu. It was he who guided the explorer on July 24, 1911 through the narrow roads and showed him parts of what today is this Majestic place.

That is where he found two peasant families living, whose surnames were Recharte and Alvarez, who used the terraces on the south side of the ruins for farming. They drank water from an Inca canal that still functioned and brought water from a spring. Pablo Recharte, one of the children of Machu Picchu, led Bingham to the "urban area" covered by weeds, while he played his quena, an Andean Wind instrument.

Bingham was very impressed by what he saw and after a short break he returned home to manage a sponsored study by Yale University, the National Geographic Society and the Peruvian Government to immediately start the studies of this citadel of stone. It was covered by a forest grown by its neglect.

Thus, with engineer Ellwood Erdis, the osteopath George Eaton, the direct involvement of Anacleto Alvarez and a group of anonymous employees of the area, he cleared this citadel of its weeds. This was a process that lasted about 3 years from 1912 to 1915. During this period they dug up many graves and found that 75 percent of the skeletons were female. This suggested that the city could have been a refuge for the Virgins of the Sun of Cusco. After an article in National Geographic Magazine in 1913, this place entered the public life and was known throughout the world.

It is important and that it is quite clear that Bingham did not discover Machu Picchu in the strict sense of the word (no one did since it was really never "lost".) Their participation and studies were important so that Machu Picchu may be known over time with publications and findings. Today there is a controversy of the very irregular exit of archaeological material of approximately 46,332 pieces. Part of this was returned to Peru in 2011, after a long struggle of the Peruvians and its government.

Machu Picchu in the Quechua language means "Old Mountain" and it is the contemporary name given to a Llaqta Inca Andean town built of stone. This citadel joins the impressive mountains of Machu Picchu and Huayna Picchu in the eastern slopes of the Central Andes in Southern Peru.

According to documentation and history, this ancient citadel was built by the Inca Pachacutec (restorer of the world) and it is the most impressive city in regards to the ceremonial as well as the centrality and access to other small towns in its surroundings that are still in the process of being cleared and which may hold many undiscovered mysteries.

This citadel is on the UNESCO World Heritage List since 1983, as part of the whole cultural and ecological, and is known under the name of The Historical Sanctuary of Machu Picchu. On the July 7th, 2007, Machu Picchu was declared as one of the new wonders of the world in a ceremony in Lisbon, Portugal, with the participation of a hundred million voters from around the world.

Machu Picchu is located in the Urubamba Canyon. Note the curve the river describes in the mountains around Machu Picchu and Huayna Picchu. The mountains are part of a large mountain formation known as Vilcabamba Batholith in the Central Mountain Range of the Andes.

These are located on the left bank of what is the Urubamba Canyon where the Willka Mayu or sacred river flows, formerly known as the Creek of Picchu, whose shrine is located halfway between the tops of the mountains. It is 450 meters above the level of the valley and 2,438 above sea level. The floor area is approximately 530 meters long by 200 wide, with approximately 200 buildings in its urban area. It is located 70 km northwest of the city of Cuzco.

To reach this citadel by one of its path you need to start on the railway line. This trail of more than 400 years of history has different entrances: one on Km 82, in Qorihayrachina or in Km 104 in Calchabamba.

The Inca paths were the only access to the sacred city of Machu Picchu in the Tahuantisuyo times with about 40 kilometers distance starting at Km 82 up to the citadel of Machu Picchu. One walks by a few lakes and along the snow capped mountains.

One enters by the beautiful ruins of Sayacmarca (3,580 m.s.l). Then you come to Puyupatamarca, the City of Clouds (3,640 m.s.l), after first seeing from above the town of Aguas Calientes. Finally, you descend to the ruins of Wiñaywaina at 2,650 m.s.l. This is the gateway to Machu Picchu.

It is a wonderful experience when you first see the citadel. The sensation of crying or yelling is the same as our ancestors felt on their pilgrimage to these villages or valleys. They did this to share their energy with nature. This path takes about 3 to 4 days, taking steps up to 4,215 m.s.l to the likes of Warmi Wanusca, Dead Woman. Other roads previously existed, which today are the train tracks that cover approx. 32 KM and that reach the town of Machu Picchu from KM 82.

The climate is warm and humid during the day and cool at night. The temperature ranges between 12 and 24 degrees Celsius. It usually rains in this area (about 1,955 mm per year), especially between November and March. The copious rains alternate rapidly with periods of intense sunshine.

Importantly, Machu Picchu had 200 homes but with a mobile population like most of the Inca villages. It varied between 300 and 1,000 people belonging to an elite class (possibly members of the panaca of Pachacutec) and Acllas. Excavations uncovered many mummies belonging to more women than men. They also discovered that the agricultural force consisted of colonies of mitimaes or mitmas (mitmaqkuna), of previously dominated different Quechua towns.

Machu Picchu was not from any point of view an isolated complex, so the myth of the "lost city" and "safe house" of the Inca Emperors lacks strength to its story.

The Incas built many administrative centers there, like temples, to cover everyone who worked on their land. To have a closer reach with the people, they built tambos and very important sacred places like Patallacta and Quente Marca, as well as abundant agricultural complexes formed by agricultural terraces.

These small populations contributed significant amounts of food to the people of Machu Picchu, because the fields in the agricultural sector of the city would be insufficient to supply the population. The roads were very important for communication and to supply any city or tambo no matter their far distance.

It is to say that Machu Picchu for its importance had to be surrounded by many villages and be strategically located. Actually it may have been a great university of which the art of organization of societies was taught. The energy of this place is awesome for the presence of more women than men suggests that it was a place of learning – a female college as its close proximity to Wiñay Huayna, which was somehow also a college for men. Both were located too far away to have a pure concentration of what they do in their various branches and functions.

The architecture used to build the city of Machu Picchu is amazing. These architects and scientists used a particular style for their buildings based on huge dimensions, monoliths and stone blocks, which were polished so that the joints between one block to another is impossible to place a pin in.

In Machu Picchu, the use of the wheel was not necessary because the quarries were found in almost the entire complex. This facilitated their transport to nearby places, with possibly the use of ramps and other tools. But to this day it is a mystery what medium was used to transport the huge blocks of stone which weighed tons.

Machu Picchu will always be a sanctuary for its large ceremonial presence in a religious and magical way. It was a peaceful city made for meditation where rituals were performed with the precious Coca and other sacred items from the edge of the jungle and the mountains. It was also where the presence of the Aclla Huasis was. In about the year 1565, the wise permanently left without any explanation. The so-called City of Peace was vacated and the jungle devoured it almost entirely, hiding it for hundreds of years.

It is said that the area known by settlers as Hera was not the citadel. José Tamayo Herrera, a known Peruvian historian, says the assumption that the area of Machu Picchu was not known during the colonial times is totally false. José Uriel García argues that he discovered an ancient script which Doña Manuela Almirón and Villegas sold the places called Picchu, Machu Picchu and Wayna Picchu on August 8, 1776 to Pedro Antonio de Ochoa for 350 pesos. Antonio de Ochoa, in turn, resold them in 1782 to Marco Antonio de la Camara for 450 pesos.

This city is part of the four suyos that were composed by Chichaisuyo, on the North of Peru and Ecuador; Collasuyo, covering Lake Titicaca, Bolivia, Chile and parts of Argentina; Antisuyo, consisting of the eastern Amazon, and Contisuyo, the western region of Cuzco.

Agriculture was the basis of the foundation of the Empire. Everyone worked with the land. Even the Emperor participated by symbolically plowing with a golden plow at the beginning of the sowing season.. The great agricultural production allowed members of the empire to maintain the large quantities of work throughout the Tahuantinsuyo aimed at building roads, bridges, temples, tambos, universities of stone and much more. The sacred towns of Machu Picchu, Ollantaytambo, Vilcabamba and others allow us to realize the love they had devoted to the concern of preserving nature and visualizing the future for its generations in the form of peace and spiritual greatness.

The large number of terraces for cultivation in Machu Picchu and the whole region establishes that the agricultural production greatly exceeded the demand of the villagers. Many archaeologists suggest that the role of the city was to provide coca leaves for the priests and royalty.

The entrance to the city was by the agricultural sector. The terraces end up in the dry ditch. Behind it you can find this city. If you continue straight you reach the end of the fountains. In reality it is a sector of 16 small water fountains, very close to the Temple of the Sun. This is a tower that has the best masonry construction throughout the city. The adjacent building, known as the Palace, was the residence of an important person.

Next to the Temple of the Sun, there is a house called huayranas or open houses. It is often called the caretaker's house of the Fountains. The structures that are directly opposite the Temple of the Sun have been classified as the Royal Sector. At the top of the terraces, a hut stands alone, a special place to get an overview of the complex. A few meters away there is a curiously shaped stone carving, known as the Funeral Rock, where mummies where prepared, then buried or taken to different places of rest. At the top of the city, one can find the Temple of Three Windows, the Main Temple. After ascending a hill you will reach the most important shrine, the Inti Watana (sundial), a sculpture of unique beauty.

At the top of Huayna Picchu, a granite peak located north of the city, is a steep path of original Inca steps, which guides you on some ramp-like structures that absorb much of the effort of climbing that the ancients felt. But the way you have to climb is slowly and with great respect as there are many cliffs. After passing the terraces, which were surely used as gardens, you reach the top where you can enjoy a spectacular view of the bird shaped city.

VILCABAMBA

This name is a composition of Vilca - coming from the native word for "huilco", the Anadenanthera colubrine tree with hallucinogenic properties that the Inca and other people who have inhabited these areas considered magical and sacred. Currently, this tree is almost extinct except for in reserves in some areas. Bamba is a modification of "pampa", bare ground or valley. Vilcabamba, therefore, means huilco valley or sacred valley.

These are the last 4 Incas who lived in this sacred place; 1537-1545: Manco Inca Yupanqui, 1545-1558: Sayri Túpac, 1558-1570 :Titu Cusi Yupanqui, 1570-1572: Túpac Amaru I, who were successors of Atahualpa who was killed by the Spanish. These also faced the dismantling of the Inca Empire by the conquerors.

They considered themselves the heirs of Huayna Capac, and was said that they first established agreements with the colonial rulers because they also faced the mistakes Atahualpa committed against these people in the civil war and against his brother Huascar. Once Atahualpa had died, his people wanted a truce with Francisco Pizarro but were only surprised to learn that they only wanted the wealth of the whole Tawantinsuyo that was informed to them by various sources that was first given as a support when they first entered Cusco.

There were still three regions in power with Atahualpa's army scattered in different regions of the empire. These were led by generals Rumiñahui, Chalcuchímac and Quisquis and were not popular with the Andean population. The political situation in the Andes at the time was unusually complicated and still to today is difficult to explain and understand.

That is why the Spanish saw the need to maintain the institution and organizations of the Incas in order to access all of its ambitions. Following the atrocities that were committed after obtaining power, they felt afraid of the Andes and its complicated geography. So they named as interim Sapa Inca a brother of Atahualpa, who was like a puppet in the actions and decisions they took. But this young man died suddenly shortly after the march Pizarro, his men and his new Andean allies (chachapoyas, huancas y cañaris, mainly) started from Cajamarca to Cuzco.

At that time Manco Inca's only intention was to restore power to the Empire with the help of the Spanish. It is clear that it only served the purposes and ambitions of the Spanish. He received the Mascay Pacha or crown of Francisco Pizarro in 1534 thus becoming a puppet ruler.

Manco Inca, on reaching the outskirts of Cusco, fought with Diego de Almagro and the captains of the Chachapoyas, Huancas and Cañaris against General Quisquis, who still maintained control of Cusco but was defeated by the powers of all of these armies who were wrong in supporting the invaders. In 1536 and after the constant looting of the capitol city, Manco Inca openly confronted the Spanish for their constant demands and abuses to get the gold and silver.

Also for the intolerance the Spanish showed towards the local beliefs and religious rituals, Manca Inca decided to plan an escape to later lead the rebellion and training in Vilvabamba. First, he promised Hernando Pizzaro to bring solid gold statues the size of a person. He said that they were in the Sacred Valley of the Incas in temples difficult to access and so was then able to leave the city.

Once in the valley, he summoned a large army of men and women to recover the plundered villages by these tyrants. He then led the army to fight in Saqsayhuaman. It was precisely here where the battle was fought, the same place the Quechuas lost at the hands of Manco Inca.

Sayri Túpac and Titu Cusi Yupanqui failed and were killed for wanting to have friendly relations with the Spanish and for having negotiations behind the backs of the Vilcabamba kingdom. They should have defended Vilcabamba for its legacy and for their Father's customs and the future of their civilization.

Then Titu Cusi's youngest brother took the realms of the Vilcabamba Kingdom. His name was Túpac Amaru I, or Fire Serpent. He faced the Spanish who were abusing the inhabitants of the valleys and mountains of this rich and vast territory.

This is where Diego de Ortiz died and this news reached the Spanish authorities. This was used as a pretext to stop all negotiations with the new Toledo Viceroy. The military was then sent (led by Martin García Óñez de Loyola) to occupy this place. Informed by spies who were often sent by the Spanish, they were then able to reach and enter Vilcabamba, and burn and destroy Vitcus. They captured the young Tupac Amaru I. He was taken to Cusco where he did not receive a fair trial. He was beheaded in 1572, and officially conquering what was of interest to the Spanish.

Vilcabamba is the only place in the world where you can give more years to life and more life to years, because the expression of its buildings are in a sense very favorable for inspiration.

Potosi - Bolivia have been found and recorded 11 Rock art sites, with many different representations clearly belonging to different periods.

Kalasasaya Temple Tiwanaku: spiritual and political center of this culture.

God of staff. This icon of the Andes has long represented the first philosophies known by the Incas, the Wari and Tiwanaku and their ancestors.

The ancient inhabitants of the lake, they knew that Lake Titicaca itself was shaped like a cat or Puma.

The Mysterious Nazca Lines and Paracas Candelabra - Peru.

The beauty of Amantani is also the beautiful flower called kantu. Today it is considered the national flower of Peru.

In Amantani and Taquile, take important issues between women and men.

Boats built of reeds, transportation and exchange served as food.

Carved in Stone of Pukara, mythical beings.

As pack animals, our ancestors used the llamas and alpacas.

142

The wool of llamas and alpacas for tissues such as coats and blankets.

Wiraqocha Temple - Racchi, one of the most beautiful buildings, which combines giant Adobe Stone worked very well Cell Type.

Cusco had the shape of a Puma, which was regarded as the special deity.

View Saqsayhuaman after the rains. Save energy a wonderful connection with the heart and mind of Mother Earth.

Stones 12, 13 and 14 angles, located in the palace of Inca Roca - Cusco.

Manco Capac, with his consort Mama Ocllo. God sent by the Sun (Inti).

Las Cuatro estrellas vista de Ollantaytambo, forma de cometa llamada Cruz del Sur, simbolizada con la Cruz andina o la Chacana.

Perolniyoc, inspiration and connection to the water which falls as a medicine for the soul. As you approach, it turns you into a new being in the water, with the energy and protection to climb a mountain.

The Sun Temple of Ollantaytambo, shown by the shadow of a feline profile, which is observed on June 21, feast of the Sun.

In Ollantaytambo, one of the most unique and amazing artwork made by the old men and women of the past, is the Temple of the Sun and giant monoliths of pink granite and red porphyry.

Staging of "Drama Ollantay", every June 29th in Ollantaytambo.

Sources Ollantaytambo ceremonial opening and closing, for the use of medicinal plants.

In Machu Picchu one feels the symbiosis of man and the Andes Mountains.

These rocks contain fine carved royal mausoleum of Machu Picchu.

151

The Temple of the Sun, a tower that has the best masonry construction across the city.

Temple of Three Windows, symbolic representation of the sacred number 3.

Source for ceremonial use in Vilca Bamba, Part of Hispanic Ñusta.

The perfect cut of the stone in Nusta Hispanic, Vilca Bamba.

Vilcabamba, the only place in the world where you can give more years to life and life to years, because the expression of its buildings, its flora and fauna are very favorable for inspiration